# A Life Behind the Scenes: from Pinewood to Hollywood

The insider diaries of
Hollywood's man in London

**Paul Hitchcock**

with

Gareth Owen

A Life Behind the Scenes: From Pinewood to Hollywood



Published in the USA by:
BearManor Media
P O Box 71426
Albany, Georgia 31708
www.bearmanormedia.com

Printed in the United States of America
ISBN 978-1-59393-895-6 (paperback)
978-1-59393-896-3 (hardcover)

Book & cover design and layout by Darlene & Dan Swanson • www.van-garde.com

Paul Hitchcock served his film apprenticeship with the Rank Organisation at Pinewood Studios, in their production budgeting department between 1946 and 1962, during the golden period of the studio when it produced films including the Norman Wisdom and *Doctor* comedies, *Genevieve, A Night To Remember* and *Northwest Frontier* to name but a few.

Leaving to go freelance, Paul began working for United Artists on five productions until, in 1966, he was head-hunted by Paramount Pictures to oversee their entire international production arm.

Subsequently as "Head Of International Production" for Warner Bros., between 1969 and 1992, he oversaw scores of movies ranging from *Gorillas In The Mist, Superman I & II, Batman* (1989), *Full Metal Jacket, Empire Of The Sun, Outland, Barry Lyndon, A Clockwork Orange, Firefox, Little Shop of Horrors* to *Greystoke.* Setting up films, doing deals and sorting out all the problems were among Paul's daily tasks.

Plus there were the films that never quite made it into production, such as David Lean's version of *The Bounty* and his ill-fated *Nostromo,* and a multi-million dollar biopic of Polish President Lech Wałęsa which the studio believed would be the "next *Driving Miss Daisy*".

Later as an independent Producer and Executive Producer he helmed films such as *First Knight, Mission Impossible I & II, The Saint, The Man in the Iron Mask, Phantom Of The Opera* and *Fred Claus.*

With a unique insight into the American studio system, Paul Hitchcock was one of Britain's most in-demand producers.

Now, for the first time, he lifts the lid on his fascinating career and times.

A few years ago Hollywood producer Robert Evans introduced me, socially, to octogenarian Sumner Redstone, the billionaire owner of Paramount Pictures, CBS and Viacom.

After our brief meeting, he said, *"Before you go Mr. Hitchcock, is there anything you would do that perhaps we're not doing at Paramount right now?"*

*"If I was running the studio Mr. Redstone, there is one thing,"* I replied, *"I'd never start a movie until I had the finished script in my hand."*

*"Do they do that?"* he asked worriedly.

I smiled widely and bid him a pleasant evening.

- Paul Hitchcock

# Contents

# Acknowledgements

First and foremost, I have to thank my wife Lidia for encouraging me to sit down and pen these memoirs. I'd always resisted, mainly because I didn't think anyone would be interested, but once I started I found the whole experience to be hugely enjoyable in recounting the many friends, colleagues, far off places and movies I'd been involved with. It made me realise just how lucky I've been.

I would also like to thank Gareth Owen for helping me collate my memories; Iris Harwood for proof reading; and Ben Ohmart and all at Bear Manor Media for publishing them!

In addition to the photographs from my own personal collection, I would like to acknowledge Robin Harbour, Alan Tomkins and Dave Worrall (at Cinema Retro magazine) for helping supply others.

Finally I'd like to pay tribute to the many crews, technicians, actors and executives who have been a part of my life and career.

John Woo and Paul (centre) on set Mission Impossible 2

# Foreword

I am very fortunate to have had the pleasure of working with a man like Paul. While making *Mission: Impossible 2,* Paul's professionalism and vast knowledge of the film business helped steer us through quite a few challenges. He is a true gentleman, always greeting you with a warm and open heart. Without his clever wit and sense of humour, there would be no joy in the art of film-making.

-John Woo

# Preface

There are many factors which determine why a film may be 'green lit' and put into production by a major US studio: they might have purchased the rights to a best-selling book; or perhaps they might have developed a story based around a true life news event which they 'optioned' from the subject involved; or maybe a particular actor or director they want to work with pitches a script they have been personally developing. Then there is the agent, friend, or family member with a personal connection who manages to 'sell' the idea of a story or script; but there is also the unexplained and totally unknown reason why a project appears on the production radar that is so uncommercial, unviable and dreadful that nobody should touch it - but guess what, it gets picked up!

"It seemed like a good idea at the time," may be the eventual excuse offered when it bombs at the box office. Some films merely try to capitalise on a genre, theme or success of another studio's project, such as when *Star Wars* was a hit every head of production started adding space movies to their development programme. Fashions and fads aren't new, there was a period when Westerns were the movies to make, then WWII films were all the rage, and nowadays in the wake of the more recent *Twilight* movie success, it seems vampires are back in vogue again. And so it will continue...

There is great originality in the US studio system with some terrific films being made, but there is also a cautiousness and concern which results in many sequels being made too, and so many classic films being 're-imagined'. You see, one of the biggest expenses involved in film-making is actually the marketing and selling of the finished film - those huge billboards, TV slots, magazine adverts and buses plastered with posters don't come cheap. So once a studio has established a title, or a character, it's something they don't need to start advertising quite so heavily second time around, as people are already familiar and their subconscious is aware. That's why so many sequels are commissioned, even if the first film was only moderately successful.

Nowadays it's becoming a business more focussed on brands and establishing a franchise, whereas when I started my career within the studio system it was more about the stars and their appeal. Certain stars could 'open a film' so you knew if you had the likes of a Gregory Peck, a Marlon Brando or a Bette Davis for example, then you were pretty much guaranteed a return, and probably a profit, on your investment. Whilst there are still stars today with that pull, Tom Cruise being one for instance, there aren't *that* many. I so fondly remember seeing queues around the block at my local Odeon of people waiting to see 'the new Clint Eastwood film' - it didn't really matter what the story or genre was, it was a Clint film and that was the appeal. I'm not so sure audiences would queue to see the new 'Joe Bloggs' film today, regardless of its genre; they're more interested in basing their decisions on seeing a new space film, a new comic book adaptation or a new special-effects loaded explosion, car chase film. Younger audiences (which make up the bulk of the box office) are not quite so fussed about 'who is in it', and that has resulted in a shift from the old star system when now no one star absolutely guarantees a studio a hit film. Sure, their name above the title helps, but it's no longer the sole deciding factor in green-lighting $200 million movies!

In my role as International Head of Production, first at Paramount and then at Warner Bros., I was responsible for overseeing some 200 feature productions from the late 1960s to the early 1990s, when I became a freelance producer.

Many of the studio films I was assigned to were co-productions with foreign partners and my involvement was much more limited in those cases; and the great majority of most films I oversaw ran like clockwork with no issues, no headaches and all came in, by and large, close on budget and schedule - so there's not a great deal I can say about them. However there were a number of films, and indeed personalities, where I do have quite a lot to share and in selecting some of those more interesting years and notes from my 50-odd years in the business, I hope to offer readers an insider's perspective to the films, deals and the people involved.

Film budgets have escalated to massive proportions. If I were to tell you the average studio budget in 1969 was around $500,000 to $5 million, whereas now they are $150 million to $200 million you can see how things have changed, and certainly how much higher the risks are. Though of course the rewards are higher too, with movies now breaking through the $1 billion recoupment level. It's a golden egg that everyone is in pursuit of.

Acclaimed screenwriter William Goldman once said, 'Nobody knows anything' when talking about movies. It's true, you can't manufacture a surefire hit - as many bankrupt production companies will testify. However, if you're careful to line up a good script, a good director and some talented actors then you stand a reasonable chance of appealing to the cinema going nation. But that said, you just never know!

It's a hugely exciting business that's for sure, and quite a glamorous one too. But then there are the aspects that you simply would not believe possible...

The famous Pinewood Double Lodge entrance

# 1946-1950

## *Welcome to Pinewood*

The first few years of my childhood were happy and fairly uneventful ones, but when war was declared on Germany I, like so many other children, was evacuated from London into the country. Now, I'm only telling this little story because years later I told director John Boorman who said, "I wish I'd known that, as I'd have put it in *Hope And Glory*."

Anyhow, clutching my gasmask and little suitcase I said goodbye to Mum and Dad and was sent off to Devon. I got off the train in Exeter and was picked up, along with 30 others, by a bus and taken to the village hall in Topsham, where on one side of the room all us children lined up and on the other the prospective 'foster parents' waited. When my name was called, a slim, spiky lady with what I've always considered to be a stereotypical spinster-like harsh face stood up, took my arm and walked me down the High Street to her terraced cottage. It was beautifully kept and full of ornaments and brasses.

"Wait here. I'm going upstairs to sort your room and I'll call you when you can come up with your case," she said sternly. Oh, how I longed to be back home with my kindly mum!

I stood in the lounge and soon noticed, on a shelf on the mantelpiece, a little brass bell. I picked it up and rattled it, but it didn't ring - the lead weight shot off and went straight through the lounge window!

I'd only been there three minutes.

The lady ran downstairs, shouting that she'd "heard about you hooligans from London" and that she'd never really wanted to take anyone in. Within 15 minutes I was back in the hall again with my little case firmly in hand.

In the end I was allocated to a couple who ran a farm, and I stayed with them for a year. They were gorgeous people and I loved spending time in the fields, picking fruit and riding on the tractor. It was quite fortunate I'd picked the bell up after all.

Anyhow, after a year the 'phoney war' period passed and it was considered safe to return to London. Well, I arrived back just in time to witness to full force of the Luftwaffe and the Blitz.

One night my mother, father, sister and I (my younger brother hadn't been born at that time), were in the underground shelter and heard the most almighty bang outside. A bomb had dropped directly on our street and our lovely house in Fulham had been flattened. Thankfully a friend of my father's found us temporary accommodation in Bourne End, Buckinghamshire and a short while afterwards the council found us a permanent new home and relocated us to Hillingdon, on the outskirts of London. It's just about as far as the Piccadilly tube line runs.

I was only about nine or ten, so the move didn't really cause me any great upheaval - young children are very adaptable I find - and I went to school locally and soon made new friends.

My father was the pianist at the Uxbridge and District Operatic Society in his spare time, and as a result was quite friendly with the music teacher at my school, who was also part of the group. I can't say I was one of his favourite nor most talented pupils, but because of his friendship with Dad, and knowing I was fourteen and fast approaching school leaving age, he said one day, "A good friend of mine has a job at Pinewood Studios and he's looking for a reliable young lad to start in the office with him. Do you think Paul would be interested?"

I was quite good at maths, and liked to think I was fairly bright, so when Dad asked me the same question, I said, "Yes, of course I'd be interested." I never really thought about exactly what I'd be doing if I'm honest, let alone imagining it might be the start of a 60-year career in the movie business!

An interview was arranged, though the studio personnel department insisted I be accompanied by one of my parents and as my dad was working Mum came with me. I remember we got the bus to Iver Heath and then walked the mile-long stretch of Pinewood Road up to the famous Double Lodge entrance.

**I'm off to play for Iver Heath Rovers FC**

We were escorted in to see the office manager called Zephaniah Harris - the only time I've even met a man whose name began with 'Z' - I later discovered it was the name of a prophet in the Bible, how prophetic for me! He told me what my duties would be in the accounts office, adding, "You have to go to night school on Tuesdays and Thursdays," and, after pausing, smiled widely and said, "Paul, starting this week is going to be very good for you."

"How's that sir?" I asked.

"Well very few people start on a short week – it's Good Friday at the end of the week, and then Easter Monday, so you'll have two four-day weeks."

I quite liked the idea of that! Though back then we also had to work on Saturday mornings from 9am until 1pm, so future weeks weren't quite as easy-going.

When people ask me, "How did you start in the business Paul?" I can honestly say it's thanks to my Dad knowing the school's music master.

Pinewood had only recently re-opened after the war, when it had been requisitioned by the Army, RAF and Crown Film Units along with housing The Royal Mint and Lloyds of London. Its parent company The Rank Organisation, headed by Chairman J. Arthur Rank - a Methodist and flour magnate - had remained busy at its other studio just down the road at Denham, but now it was swinging back into full production at its Iver Heath dream factory. And it was a bit of a dream for me because I was a regular at the local cinema with my Dad; we'd go at least once a week, but because it was so busy in those days we were never sure if we'd get in – we'd go to the Odeon in Uxbridge, for example, and see they were queuing around the block so then we'd dodge across to the Regal or the Savoy.

I was tremendously interested in getting a job at Pinewood, which I suppose could be best described as a cross between an industrial estate with all sorts of trucks and trailers dropping off their loads of tubular steel, plywood sheets and bags of plaster, and a gentile country estate. It had a grand stately home, Heatherden Hall at its centre and about 100 acres of land spreading out from around it. Everything a production needed was either found on site, or could be made there. The carpenters' shop whined with buzz saws slicing through timber, and a few days later it'd be propped up by some tubular scaffolding with a bit of plaster over it, becoming a London Mews house, or the bridge on a British war ship. The smell of paint, timber and the heat from the huge arc lamps had a uniqueness about it that I've never experienced anywhere else outside of a film studio and still excites me when I walk past a stage.

Then of course there were the film stars! In the lunch hour on my first day I wandered up to the lot and saw they were doing something on a film called *Green For Danger* with Alistair Sim. It was pretty exciting stuff. It was a year or so before the main restaurant in the grand ballroom re-opened, and from then on I'd see all manner of actors and stars passing my office window daily, on their way to lunch.

I was based in the accounts department where I was surrounded by huge ledgers, in which I noted the 'charge-outs'. You see, everyone on the Rank payroll, be they a cameraman, carpenter, painter, electrician or actor, was paid a weekly wage and those wages were all charged against productions whenever possible. So, for example, if I, Paul Hitchcock was assigned to a film shooting on the lot for 6 weeks, I'd have to be entered into the ledgers with the number of hours I'd worked each day recorded. Then the Rank accounts people would total it all up and invoice the production - plus a bit on top I dare say.

Every week I had to work my way through these many ledgers and tot up the exact amounts in each column - two hours here, three days there and so forth. There were no adding machines, and calculators were many years away from being invented. I have to admit it was quite daunting at first, as there was I, a young lad armed only with an ink pen ensuring Britain's biggest film company received what was due. If you ever made a mistake you'd have to take a razor blade and gently scratch away the ink to write over it with the correct figure. But I enjoyed maths, and without wanting to sound conceited, it soon all came to me quite easily.

Everyone at the studio had to wear a shirt, tie and jacket – unless it was exceptionally hot in the summer, when you were allowed to take your jacket off – so there was certainly an air of formality about the place, but there was also a sense of being involved in a rather magical industry.

One of my saddest memories dates back to Whit Bank Holiday Monday in 1948 when I was playing tennis with my Dad on my day off, and he was a pretty accomplished player, but afterwards in the evening he complained that he felt terribly, terribly tired and thought he had tonsillitis coming on – which was something my Mother had experienced – and in fact it reached the point where he didn't even have the strength to climb the stairs to bed. My Mother made a make-shift bed up for him downstairs and from that day on he never walked again. He had in fact contracted polio and spent the next six months in an iron lung, and then spent a further year in Stanmore Orthopaedic Hospital where he was told he'd be in a wheelchair for the rest of his life. It affected the household hugely, of course, as with Dad being unable to work my modest wage coming in was all-important and I grew up very fast.

For four years I happily kept the ledgers at Pinewood and earned an honest crust; and I'd like to think I did a fair job of it.

My colleagues in the RAF

My station cricket team, during National Service

# 1950-1952

## *Duty Calls*

Aged eighteen, my army call-up papers arrived for National Service. I knew it was coming, as immediately post-World War II, it was expected of every able-bodied young man to give eighteen months of his life to training and to help thwart any potential invasion. I say eighteen months, but no sooner had I signed up with the RAF than it was increased to two years!

I became a clerk in the Station Warrant Officer's Office, and moved around to places like Driffield, Leighton Buzzard and finally Ruislip for a short time. Up until that time I'd never really been away from home, and I know it's a bit of a cliché, but it really did teach you discipline and when you were told to get up at 5am, you got up at 5am.

Mind you I found if you played sport, and I played cricket and football, then you had the most wonderful time as you were able to travel to matches and it got you away from the more mundane parades, guard duties and other menial tasks.

Speaking of football, I've always supported Fulham FC which is no doubt partly to me being Fulham-born myself, and see them play whenever I can. When war was declared all league football was later cancelled, so I only saw a few games, but I became a regular again in 1945. I mention this because, ironically, having supported the club for over seventy years I only recently discovered, after my daughter-in-law started tracing the Hitchcock family tree, that my great grandfather James Hitchcock was Chairman of Fulham Football Club when they were playing in the Southern league and, in 1903, initiated the approach to gain entry to Division One! He was a Director from 1903 until 1905, the year when he passed away.

I found it most odd that no one in my family ever mentioned my great grandfather's involvement. Had they done, it may have meant a discount on my season ticket!

Back in army life, when people were demobbed I had to fill in a whole load of forms about their skills, training, where they were going to live and so on. When I told the officer in charge that I didn't really understand half of what was on the paperwork, he said, "Neither do I, I just throw them all away." So after filling them in (to the best of my ability) for a short while, I too ended up throwing them in the dustbin; I always thought if there was ever another war nobody would know how to find any of these servicemen!

There was a tacit understanding that any person enrolling in National Service should be able to return to the position and company they left prior to joining up, and companies were obliged to keep your job open. Therefore when I was finally demobbed and filled in my own forms, I contacted the Rank Organisation.

John Davis, Head of the Rank Organisation

# 1952-1962

## *Back at Pinewood*

Happily, in 1952, I was welcomed back by Rank and returned to Pinewood where I was promoted into the budgeting department, and that's when I started to learn about film budgets and scheduling. Initially I'd be given schedules by the production managers from which I'd calculate a budget, but as my understanding of them grew I'd actually draw up my own to see how it compared with the production manager's.

It certainly proved to give me a terrific grounding for what was to lie ahead in my career, as I developed a very good understanding of budgets, schedules and how they were put together from a script... and how the 'front office' would then beat them down in order to make what they felt was an affordable risk!

Rank's films were all fairly modest budget affairs - John Davis later decreed nothing costing more than £150,000 would be made - because they knew, on the whole, they'd need to recoup their costs from the home market. They usually did too. *Doctor In The House* made by Betty Box and Ralph Thomas made its money back in six weeks at the Odeon Leicester Square, and nationwide it was calculated 17 million admissions were made at the box office to see it. Beyond the UK some films fared well, but other more parochial subjects didn't travel successfully. So I learned about commerciality and box office considerations too.

**Genevieve, the film no one wanted to make became one of the most fondly regarded Pinewood movies**

Rank was producing a huge number of films at that time including *Genevieve* - which, curiously, head of production Earl St. John wasn't at all keen on making, yet it became their most successful and affectionately regarded film - the Norman Wisdom comedies, starting with *Trouble In Store,* and the aforementioned *Doctor* comedies with Dirk Bogarde to name but a few.

Rank fully financed the movies, and as they owned their own distribution company and Odeon cinemas, they were really the UK's nearest thing to the US studio system.

Arthur Alcott was the studio controller, and ultimately my boss. He'd allocate me to certain films, give me a script or a book to schedule and budget. There were six or eight of us in the department, costing up projects, and if they were given the go-ahead I'd then work alongside the production manager and that's how I got to know such great people as Charles Orme,

Denis Holt and Hugh Attwooll. I would never interfere in the creative side of things, but would of course keep an eye on the daily and weekly costs.

I worked on most of the Norman Wisdom films, a huge number of the Betty Box-Ralph Thomas productions including *The Iron Petticoat, Checkpoint, The Wind Cannot Read, A Tale of Two Cities* and other productions like *Hell Drivers* with Stanley Baker and Sean Connery (who I think was billed about sixth), *Ferry To Hong Kong* with Orson Welles, followed by *Northwest Frontier* with Lauren Bacall - who was brought in by Rank in an attempt to compete with American films - but they didn't do the extra business to warrant that big-star expense.

Anyhow, I'd visit the stages daily when they were shooting and, under strict instruction to never allow a film to overrun its usual six or seven week schedule, or go beyond its agreed budget, I'd report back any situations I thought might be problematic. I'd like to think although I was the eyes and

**Doctor in the House, the first film in the series**

**Earl St John (left) who was head of production for Pinewood, here talking with contract director Roy Ward Baker**

ears of the studio, I had good working relationships with all the producers on the lot.

I might, for example, see two camera cranes on set one day when I knew only one had been budgeted for, so would have a word with the production manager who would say, "Oh we've just brought it in for a couple of hours."

Well, that was an overage that had to be accounted for and so I'd look for them to compensate for it in another scene and they might then, for instance, say rather than build an office set for scene 32, they'd find one near the studio that they could use and save money there. That was all fine. The main thing was nothing could be improvised in terms of bringing in extra equipment, unless it could be paid for from within the existing budget. When you think John Davis, the feared head of the Organisation, placed

**Trouble In Store, Norman Wisdom's first film for Rank**

an upper limit of £150,000 on any film, there wasn't any room for overages; particularly with three films shooting at any one time.

There were a huge number of actors and film-makers under contract to Rank, and the story department worked flat-out throughout the year looking for prospective stories and scripts. But no matter how successful a star and film, like the Norman Wisdom ones for instance, the company wouldn't want to spend any more on a sequel; they wanted it for the same price. That

**Doctor At Large, on location shooting with director Ralph Thomas behind the camera**

proved challenging. But they were right as the domestic market was limited.

Every week, financial reports were sent up to London for John Davis to see and I remember the cost statements for each week had to be on his desk the following Tuesday at 10am. There'd then be a call asking, "Why has this film spent an extra £2000 on sets?" or "What is the reasoning for working overtime?" and so on. They weren't particularly nice phone calls!

The only time I fell foul of Davis, he fired me. It was on a film called *Windom's Way* with Peter Finch and Mary Ure, and Ronald Neame was directing. We were out on the backlot for some night shooting and it was fast developing into a disaster with torrential and constant rain meaning they were running over schedule quite badly. I went over to see producer John Bryan and said that I knew Ronnie Neame's contract, which included prep time, shooting and a few weeks afterwards, was running out.

"Don't worry Paul, I'll speak to Ronnie," John assured me, "it's only going to be another two or three weeks, he'll do it for nothing. He wants to finish the film."

Well, the film wrapped and an invoice arrived from Ronnie's agent for three more weeks' salary. I obviously hadn't allowed for anything more, and so went to see John Bryan and he sort of shrugged his shoulders. "Ronnie wouldn't have minded doing a week for nothing," he said, "but not three."

John Davis received my weekly report, saw the director's costing overage and phoned me up.

"Hitchcock! What's this?"

I explained what had happened, and he snapped, "Did you have anything in writing?"

"No, I didn't," I confessed.

"I can't put up with this," and he slammed the phone down.

Arthur Alcott had retired by this time and a chap named A. W. Robinson had taken over; I was summoned to his office.

"I'm very sorry," he said, "but John Davis wants you fired. You leave on Friday."

On the Thursday, Robinson rang me up and said, "Look, I've thought about it and you can stay."

Phew.

That same year, one of Rank's most successful films ever, *A Night To Remember*, moved on to the lot. Unfortunately it wasn't one I was assigned to, but I was very much aware of it. It brought a prestige to Rank that it had previously not enjoyed. No longer was it a company that just produced twee comedies and local dramas.

Things started changing slightly when the renters moved in, first of all Walt Disney Pictures made a number of films and then in 1958 Peter Rogers came along with a low budget comedy called *Carry On Sergeant*, which became the first of 30 other *Carry Ons* and which helped show Pinewood was a studio where affordable films could be made. The studio rented space out to producers, but of course had no involvement in scripts or budgets. However, realising they could still profit from us folks in the budgeting department, we were rented out.

I remember the first time I was assigned to a non-Rank film was in 1961 when Michael Winner made *Play It Cool,* with Billy Fury and Helen Shapiro. Talk about a baptism of fire. I think it was Winner's second film, though he was just as arrogant then as he was fifty years later! Armed with a megaphone, he barked directions at everyone on set - no matter if they were right next to him - and the crew became so fed up that Harry Black, the wonderful 'gaffer' on the movie, rubbed carbon from the lamps around the mouthpiece when the director was off the set at one point, and when he returned and started shouting his orders all of the electricians sang out, "Mammy!", in their best impressions of Al Jolson.

A lot more freelancers arrived in the studio and most of the jobs on films were actually fixed-up in the studio bar. Mind you, not just anyone could walk in there back in those days; you had to be of a certain standing and importance and, at all times, smartly dressed. Similarly with the restaurant; it was very difficult to get a table in there. Draughtsmen or prop men certainly need not have tried, for example. Tommy Thomas ran the restaurant and he was very picky as to whom he allowed in; occasionally if he needed to fill the place up a bit, you might stand a better chance but couldn't bet on it.

The disciplinarian feel also extended beyond the commissary as you weren't allowed to walk on the grass in the huge gardens. I found that out the hard way when a few of the lads and I had a football kick around one lunchtime and were told, in no uncertain terms, to clear off.

I greatly enjoyed my time at Pinewood, and met some wonderful people along the way and in December 1962 I received a call from one of the production guys I knew, who said, "Paul, I'm starting a film in January with Lewis Gilbert. Would you be interested in leaving Pinewood and coming to work with us?"

**Director Michael Winner on the set of Play It Cool**

As with most things in life, offers tend to come at the wrong time. My wife was heavily pregnant, and we were in the middle of one of the worst winters ever. With buses cancelled, I had to cycle in to work and of course felt I had to discuss it with her before making any decision. Heavy snow or not, Rank expected us to work full days. When I thought they might possibly let me go home if my wife went into labour, I was told, "Women have babies, men stay at work," but to "give her our love when you see her after work."

As you couldn't even make a phone call without someone asking what it was about, I waited until 5pm (when they let me off, thirty minutes early) to cycle home to Windsor and said, "Beryl, I'm thinking of leaving Pinewood at the end of the year and going to Kuala Lumpur."

"Where's Kuala Lumpur?" she asked. You must remember neither of us had been anywhere outside of the UK, apart from a boat trip to France once.

Although it was somewhat daunting to give up a full-time paid position to go freelance, it was an opportunity I felt I couldn't turn down - yes it was more money, and we certainly needed it now, but it was also a progression which I didn't feel I'd ever achieve if I stayed at Pinewood for another ten years, as whilst I was carrying out the duties of a production manager for Rank, I was regarded only as a glorified accountant, and I don't believe they'd have ever seen me otherwise.

Mind you in the days after I gave in my notice I went to the bathroom a lot, and didn't sleep much!

The-7th-Dawn, the working title was 'The Third Road'

# 1963

## *The Seventh Dawn*

*The Seventh Dawn* was a Malaysian-set drama with a terrific cast including William Holden, Cappucine, Susannah York and Tetsuro Tamba, and is the story of three friends from WWII ending up on opposing sides during the communist insurgency.

Bill Kirby was the production manager who'd tempted me away and to whom I reported at United Artists' Wardour Street office.

It all felt pretty good, and my worries soon evaporated. Some lunch times we'd go out to top restaurants like the White Elephant, which was a total eye-opener for me, as after all back at Pinewood I felt lucky if Tommy Thomas thought me important enough to allow me in the commissary.

Anyway, after three, or possibly four, weeks Bill said to me, "I'm leaving this picture, and they're bringing in someone else."

I felt the blood rushing from my face. "Where does that leave me?" I asked, thinking I'd just made the biggest mistake of my life.

"They're bringing in someone called John Dark," Bill said, "and he wants to meet you. He has his own assistant but will see if he thinks you can work together."

It was now a very different world.

John Dark met me for lunch, and eventually said, "OK, I'll tell you what.

**A later photograph of my friend John Dark, here producing At the Earth's Core with director Kevin Connor and cameraman Alan Hume**

We're going out to Malaya to do a recce. Come out with me and we'll see how it works out."

Roll forward a few days, and I was sitting next to John on the plane. "What's the furthest you've flown before?" he asked.

"Where are we now?"

"Just going over the Alps," he replied.

"Then just over the Alps is the furthest I've ever flown."

"Are you telling me you've never flown before?"

"Never in my life," I replied, as I turned my head to look out of the window.

John obviously thought he had some second rate idiot here, as he had a very responsible job and was used to having an experienced right-hand man with him. Working for Lewis Gilbert is one of the most pleasurable experiences ever, but it's a huge responsibility as he leaves all the planning and setting-up for you to do.

We landed in Kuwait to refuel, so John and I popped into the duty free shop. It was like an Aladdin's cave to me! Returning back to the plane, the new captain - who was joining us for the next leg - greeted us all one by one, and then I heard:

"Paul, how lovely to see you again. What are you doing here?"

I looked up and said, "Roy Copeman! What are you doing here?"

"I'm flying you to Kuala Lumpur. Once we're up, why don't you and your colleague come on up to the cockpit and we'll have a chat."

So we took our seats and then a short while after, the steward came along and asked if we'd like to join the captain.

"Paul, you've never flown before," John exploded, "and you know the fucking captain!"

**Above: My first ever overseas assignment and my first flight!**

**Director Lewis Gilbert**

JOE MOSES IS HIS NAME...
STEALING AFRICA IS HIS GAME!
So how did he inherit an elephant, a blonde and a tribe of restless natives?
He's so shy
He's so popular
He's so friendly
JOIN THIS SAFARI AND FIND OUT!
Robert Mitchum Carroll Baker
in THE FRANK ROSS PRODUCTION
"Mister Moses"
PANAVISION TECHNICOLOR
UNITED ARTISTS

Roy, the captain, used to work in the blueprint department at Pinewood when I first joined up and his father worked at Denham, so I knew the family very well. When I signed up for my national service, Roy went off to the RAF for his and stayed for three years. He could already fly as he used to go up from Denham Airfield on pleasure flights, and then from the RAF he became a commercial pilot for BOAC.

Thereafter, we kept in touch and whenever I was on location in a far flung corner of the world, Roy would inevitably have a flight there at some point, and we'd meet for dinner.

That incident cemented my friendship with John Dark too, and we developed a wonderful working relationship.

I looked forward to going to work every day on this film, and particularly with Lewis who was always incredibly well prepared and knew exactly what he was shooting - which I assure you doesn't happen very often these days, quite the contrary – I've found directors will walk on a set in the morning and only then start thinking about what they might do.

Having completed *The Seventh Dawn*, UA announced their next film was to be *Mr Moses* directed by Ronnie Neame and starring Robert Mitchum and Carroll Baker. I of course knew Ronnie from my Pinewood days, so it was a very happy reunion.

We found locations in Naivasha, which was ninety minutes' drive from Nairobi, and had the most wonderful terrain and vistas. There were no hotels anywhere between Nairobi and the location, and the only possible billet was a disused monastery which had a main building, and lots of bungalows surrounding it. So we took out a year-long lease and completely renovated the entire site, making it habitable for the crew - complete with restaurant.

During the prep period Lee Katz, who was a UA Executive in New York, called to ask me to meet Robert Mitchum at Nairobi airport, and I was to explain the accommodation wasn't a hotel but a modified monastery. So I rehearsed my little speech and arranged to drive with a car right up to the plane's steps, making our star's transit as easy as possible.

"I'm Paul Hitchcock, Mr. Mitchum," I said, "representing UA. The hotel..."

Well, he wasn't the least bit interested and the only thing he said during the drive was, "Suck what kid?"

On arriving at our accommodation I braced myself for what I thought would be a tirade of "Do you know who I am?" but, quite the contrary, he loved the bungalow we assigned to him and the freedom it gave him. There were also lots of wild animals wandering in and out of the compound, which he loved.

Mitchum had arrived before we'd actually started shooting as he'd told UA that he wanted a complete break before starting on the film, and he treated this whole period as a holiday. Sometimes, when I had to go into Nairobi, he'd ask for a lift and whilst I was at my various meetings he happily wandered around like a tourist, and later met up with me for lunch at the Norfolk Hotel which was always full of good-looking young, blond men who were referred to by the locals as the "white hunters" - and they in turn naturally thought they were God's gift to the world. One lunch time, one of the "white hunters" turned to Mitchum and said,

"You think you're tough don't you?"

He was seemingly keen to pick a fight, but Mitchum looked at him and said,

"Kid, I have sucked people like you up one nostril!" and walked off.

Once we started shooting everything ran smoothly, except on one day when we broke for lunch. The plan was to set fire to some of the Masai huts, and resume shooting after lunch, as the huts would then just be smouldering, but a special effects technician had left a gas cylinder inside one of the huts and of course it exploded. Tragically a Masai guard was killed and before we knew what had happened the catering tent was surrounded by very hostile Masai warriors all carrying spears.

It took some time, with the help of a local farmer, to negotiate with the Masai Chief some compensation for the deceased man's family. It was a terrible accident, and a tragic one at that, but once compensation had been settled and we'd done everything we could for the family, we were able to resume filming and thanks to having a very experienced director like Ronnie on board, we made up the lost time. It was a joy working with Ronnie and such a professional star as Bob Mitchum. Some of us were also invited to the uhuru freedom celebrations when Mr. Jomo Kenyatta became president of the country in 1964.

KHARTOUM – WHERE THE NILE DIVIDES,
THE GREAT CINERAMA ADVENTURE BEGINS!

CHARLTON HESTON · LAURENCE OLIVIER
as GORDON    as THE MAHDI

RICHARD JOHNSON
RALPH RICHARDSON

A JULIAN BLAUSTEIN PRODUCTION
CINERAMA

JULIAN BLAUSTEIN   ROBERT ARDREY   BASIL DEARDEN
ULTRA PANAVISION · TECHNICOLOR   UNITED ARTISTS

# 1964

## *Khartoum*

I'd just started working on *What's New Pussycat?* in Italy when the executives from United Artists (UA) rang me and asked me to move on to a picture called *Gordon of Khartoum* (later re-titled *Khartoum*).

To cut a long story short I flew out to Khartoum in Sudan, and met Lewis Gilbert - who was going to direct the movie - when, all of a sudden, a civil war broke out. From our offices we could see the American Embassy alight and Lewis, who I love dearly, could never be described as courageous because he immediately said "Darling, darling, we've got to get out of here!" which is exactly what we did that afternoon.

Back in London, we started setting the film up but Lewis, obviously mindful of Sudan being a little unpredictable, accepted another offer and went off to make *Alfie* with Michael Caine.

Our film came to a standstill.

UA were still very keen, as they thought it was a great subject, so we started looking at other potential locations in Morocco, Spain and Egypt. In fact we settled on Egypt as along with the terrain being perfect, there was a greater number of camels there, which was important to the film!

Though there was a complicating factor; our movie had to qualify as an 'Eady picture'. That is to say, under the guidelines of the 'Eady Plan' films

Charles K. Feldman presents
Peter Sellers Peter O'Toole
Romy Schneider
Capucine
Paula Prentiss
and least but not last
Woody Allen
and guest star
Ursula Andress
They're all together again!
(for the first time!)
HOW YOU CATS WILL LAUGH
when you see the answer to the comedy question of the year!!!
"What's New Pussycat?"
THIS PICTURE IS RECOMMENDED FOR ADULTS ONLY
Screenplay by WOODY ALLEN / Directed by CLIVE DONNER / Produced by CHARLES K. FELDMAN
Musical Score by BURT BACHARACH / Lyrics by HAL DAVID
TECHNICOLOR
Released thru UNITED ARTISTS

that were classified as being British qualified for certain tax relief, which was actually sizeable to the production. It was easier to qualify in Egypt than any of the other places because there was a lot of 'blocked money' there. Unlike nowadays, there wasn't free trade between countries and many major concerns such as Coca-Cola had vast profits from sales that they just couldn't get out of Egypt. UA approached one of these such companies and offered to buy their foreign assets at 50c on the $ - or every dollar they had in Egypt, UA would give them 50c back in the US. It was purely that 'blocked money' that helped finance the movie.

The Eady Plan, which was abolished in the 1980s, was actually a big contributing factor in American film-makers coming to the UK, including Albert R. Broccoli who stayed on to make the James Bond films with Harry Saltzman.

I'd suggested Basil Dearden as a potential director, as I knew him from my Pinewood days and always felt he was an immensely competent and clever man, and I was delighted when I heard he'd been recruited. The second unit was meanwhile directed by Yakima Canutt, an American rodeo rider, actor, stuntman (most notably on John Wayne's many films) and action director on movies such as *Ben Hur, El Cid* and *Spartacus.*

*Khartoum* was filmed in 65mm and the studio really were putting everything into the project, as it was set to be one of their big tent-pole releases.

Basil proved to be the perfect choice, not least when we heard Laurence Olivier, who was set to play The Mahdi, had developed a throat problem and refused to travel to Egypt; obviously we didn't want to lose Olivier in the film, as he was a big selling point, and Basil felt he would be able to shoot everything involving the character on location with a double, and then bring Olivier into Pinewood for reverse shots, close-ups and so on. I defy anybody to say Laurence Olivier wasn't in Egypt for all his scenes, as that was the genius in Basil's direction. A lesser director wouldn't even know where to start!

Burt Lancaster had been set to star as General Gordon, but after scheduling changes he dropped out and Charlton Heston played the role; I think it was one of the best films he ever made.

One of the main problems we encountered at the end of location shooting was trying to get our equipment (cranes, cameras, dollies, lights etc.) out and back to the UK. Unfortunately we discovered our shipping agent, who is today a rather well known businessman in the world, was totally corrupt! Part of the agreement with the authorities, enabling us to use the 'blocked money' in the country was that every bill incurred had to go through our Cairo local bank account; but the shipping agent wanted his fees to be paid directly to his Swiss bank account. He even arrived at the production office at Pinewood one day to plead his case, and my secretary asked to see me for a moment.

"His driver has just left a painting for you as a present," she said.

"That's nice of him," I thought and went back in and said, "I'm afraid there is no way we can pay you through Switzerland."

"Then you will have to take the consequences. I suggest you speak to UA and say there can be a saving here."

I excused myself and popped into my secretary's office and said, "Would you take the painting downstairs, give it to the driver and tell him to take it away."

United Artists agreed with me that although it would cost us several tens of thousands of dollars extra, we could not break our word with the Egyptian authorities by doing back door deals. As a consequence of our honesty the shipping agent made us wait a long time before we got our equipment back – not what you'd call nice people that's for sure.

# 1966

## *The Bells Of Hell Go Ting A Ling A Ling*

The Mirisch Company, through United Artists, had been setting up this World War I film - written by Roald Dahl and to be directed by David Miller - which was based on the true story of taking bi-planes through Switzerland on an air raid on the Zeppelin factory just over the border at Friedrichshafenm.

Gregory Peck was lined up to star, along with a (then) unknown young actor named Ian McKellen, whom Peck addressed as 'Loo-tenant' and when McKellen corrected his pronunciation, "in UK we say 'Left-tenant'," the director told him to shut up, adding "Never forget Ian, Great Britain is only 5% of the world market."

On arriving at the production office in Switzerland, I was presented with a budget and schedule and, having read the script, simply said, "This isn't possible!"

Someone had drawn up a totally unrealistic budget, then left the production. No doubt that's why I was parachuted in.

I came up with a revised, and more expensive, budget which - somewhat reluctantly - UA agreed to. All the preparation and location scouting was done in the winter months, but as we fast approached summer, there was no snow - as it has a habit of melting in the warmer weather! To say it was a disaster would be putting it mildly.

After three weeks' shooting, we were a good ten days behind schedule and I'd been saying to Cecil Ford, who was the Mirisch rep on the movie, that in my opinion it was going to cost an absolute fortune to finish, and conservatively estimated we'd end up ten weeks over schedule. At this point we hadn't shot anything with Gregory Peck and I was very nervous about bringing Greg into a scenario where the director was having daily heart attacks trying to cope.

On the next Monday morning, having thought about it all weekend, I told Cecil that on the following Thursday I was going to phone UA and tell them I felt the project should be abandoned unless he thought otherwise. "I'd better speak to the Mirisch office then," he replied.

Tuesday and Wednesday passed without Cecil saying a word to me, though I always thought him one of the types who firmly believed the sun would shine tomorrow and all would be rosy in the garden. I remained a bit more pragmatic.

On Thursday I rang the heads of UA, Arthur Krim and David Picker, and told them what I thought and said that Cecil had spoken to the Mirisch brothers about it too; though I later discovered he hadn't at all.

"Are you sure of your facts Paul?" Arthur Krim asked.

"We're in the shit Mr. Krim," I replied.

A couple of days later Mr. Krim arrived in Gstaad, and with UA already having begrudgingly agreed to spending the extra money I'd budgeted, he was extremely unhappy about another massive overage, and so cancelled the film. Nowadays I don't think that would happen – they'd likely limp along shooting what they could, and then come back for re-shoots the following year. But I've always been of the opinion you shouldn't try and patch up a bad job, it's far better to hold your hands up and not throw good money after bad.

I had to sign an affidavit explaining the situation and that it was effectively an irretrievable production, following which the actors were paid their contractual obligations - I believe Ian McKellen, for example, has since said he was paid a rather handsome £4000 - and we all flew home. Greg Peck wasn't paid his full fee I know, and I dread to think how much that'd have been, but he was offered another picture so came away happy.

Whilst I hate to think of anyone losing a job, or a film having to be closed down, it was the only answer in this particular situation and sometimes the most difficult decision is the only practical one to take.

Mary Pickford, in one of her early starring roles.

# 1966-1969

## *The Paramount Years*

All the films I'd worked on up until now, as a freelancer, were for United Artists, and they knew I wasn't afraid to speak my mind or make difficult decisions.

Bud Ornstein was the head of UA in London and I knew him reasonably well; whilst you could say he was more on the creative side of the business than in the nuts and bolts department of working on a film set, he'd always be around for the first screening and to then oversee the PR machine. He was certainly passionate about what he did and in fact had been very much involved in the green-lighting of the James Bond films, The Beatles films, and *Tom Jones* with Albert Finney to name but a few. He was very highly regarded and respected within the business.

Anyhow, after my Swiss adventure Bud called me and said he'd left UA and had been offered the job of running Paramount Pictures in London. It was a much bigger role than he'd had at UA and in fact it would be more accurate to say he was in charge of *all* Paramount's activities outside of America. He said he was putting a team together including Michael Flint, a lawyer from Denton Hall & Bergin, as business affairs manager; as his creative assistant, a guy called Jerry Juroe - who went on to become marketing manager on the majority of Cubby Broccoli's Bond films - was coming on board, and he asked me to meet him for a chat.

I went up to Wardour Street and, cutting a long story short, Bud offered me the job as 'Head of Physical Production'. Whilst he again was happy to stay on the creative side, he wanted someone he knew and trusted to run all the productions.

As with any executive coming into a film company, Bud inherited a number of projects in different stages of development and ones that had already started production. Once he'd found his feet after a couple of months, Bud suggested I join him on a trip to LA to meet everyone at Paramount's headquarters.

"I don't stay at a hotel though," he told me, "I always stay at Pickfair, and so will you."

Pickfair, as it was dubbed by the American press, was the Beverly Hills home of Mary Pickford and Douglas Fairbanks. I think it was *Life* magazine that said it was "a gathering place only slightly less important than the White House, and much more fun."

Bud's wife was Mary Pickford's niece, and so that's why Bud liked to stay with Aunt Mary whenever he was back in town. She was also, I must add, one of the founding partners in United Artists with Charlie Chaplin, Fairbanks and D. W. Griffith, to better control their own work.

In 1976, when Mary was awarded an Honorary Oscar, they filmed her acceptance in the grand living room and it was said to be one of the few, if not the only, time it was seen on screen, yet I can imagine how many glittering showbiz parties they'd hosted there for visiting Royalty, Presidents, movie stars and family friends. Bud and I stayed in the guest bungalow in the gardens; there'd have been room in the main house too I'd think as it had over twenty rooms, tastefully decorated with English and French antique furniture. Every day we'd head across to see Aunt Mary, in her bedroom. In all the years I stayed there, I never saw her get up out of bed. In fact she had become rather reclusive and spoke to most visitors at the house only on the telephone from her bedroom. I realise I was very privileged to sit on the edge of her bed, and she'd ask me questions such as, "What is Harrod's like... is Fortnum and Mason still there... do people still go to tea at the Ritz?" and so

**Me (far right) with Charles Bludhorn, Jean-Paul Belmondo and Bud Ornstein, on set for Paramount's 'The Brain'**

on. She was incredibly curious about everything. It was quite surreal actually for this Fulham-supporting, working class lad from London to find himself sitting with one of cinema's biggest stars, and across the hall her husband, jazz musician Buddy Rogers, would sit at a piano to play for her (and me).

She told me a story one day about when she and former husband Douglas Fairbanks took a cruise to the Far East, I think for about six or eight months, after he'd just completed a western movie; she bought the actual saloon bar from the production, and had it installed in the basement at Pickfair as a Christmas present for him. I knew the bar was there as Bud had shown me around the house, but I never knew its history. Sadly it went when the house was demolished in 1990.

Anyhow, Bud and I went over to meet with Charles Bluhdorn, head of Paramount Pictures. Bluhdorn was Austrian-born; in 1926, he had moved to America aged 16 to complete his education, and by the time he was 30 he was a millionaire - all thanks to sugar trading in the Dominican Republic, and then later his involvement with a car spare parts company. He told me one night that he made his first fortune and lost it overnight but added, "I was determined to make it all again" - and he did. His company, Gulf + Western, acquired Paramount in 1966 and he had many other companies in his portfolio too including Simon & Schuster publishing. To say he was a workaholic and extremely energetic would be an understatement and, as I soon learned, he expected the same of his management. Never mind *The Wolf of Wall Street*; they called him 'The Mad Austrian of Wall Street' - and he never lost his thick German accent. He'd jump from one subject to another, and would be speaking to everybody in the room but addressing everyone individually in his mind. It was very difficult to keep up with him. Fortunately, I had Bud as a 'buffer' between us so knew I wouldn't have a great deal to do with Bluhdorn on a day-to-day basis, but alas Bud only lasted a year and left the company!

I then found myself dealing directly with Bluhdorn. He seemed to like me, and more importantly trusted my judgement, as whenever he despatched me to a film set somewhere, he'd say "it's under control now."

For instance, I was setting up *The Adventurers* (1970) with director Lewis Gilbert in Paris, but then there were a whole series of riots and we realised we had to relocate to studios in Rome. Locations included Manizales and Cartagena, in Colombia, but we set it all up in Bogotá.

Charlie phoned me and said, "Paul, I want you to go to Colombia to see how it's going." So I flew to Bogotá, then took a plane up to Manizales, only to be handed a telex from Charlie which said, "Concerned about *Downhill Racer*. Go to Kitzbühel, Austria, immediately".

I waved goodbye to Lewis and took a plane to the set of the Robert Redford-Gene Hackman film on the other side of the world, and that's how my life was for the three years I was with Paramount. If there was ever a concern or a problem on a film, Charlie would say, "Don't worry, I've sent Hitchcock there", and wherever I was or what other projects I was involved with didn't matter; so long as I was on the way, the problem was solved - in Charlie's mind at any rate. My feet honestly never touched the ground, and despite my trying to explain to Charlie that I'd have been better standing still for a while on some occasions, he never saw it that way. Consequently I felt like a fireman without water - I arrived on the scene, but could never really put any fires out properly before shooting off again. They were always short fixes.

Things reached a head when I found myself in charge of fifty-two films, shooting all around the world. Many were foreign, and quite involved, three-way co-productions, and I needed to make sure they were on schedule and budget, know when we'd take delivery and ensure co-financing agreements were honoured. I couldn't honestly begin to comprehend how I was going to oversee all these productions so I caught a plane to New York to see Charlie and said, "I think you've got the wrong guy."

"What are you talking about?"

"It's all these films. I won't possibly get time to visit them all. It's just a nightmare," I said.

"Paul, go back to London and hire as many staff as you need but make sure you get someone as good as, or better than, yourself."

I've never forgotten those words, and when I hear people saying things like, "Oh, I won't employ him as he'll be after my job" I think, "No, that's exactly the type of person you *want* to employ."

I ensured I surrounded myself with good people, and had contracts with the very best people in England. For example, Geoffrey Unsworth was, in my mind, one of our finest cinematographers, though he always had financial problems; so I offered him a three-year contract, which was unheard of at the time, but I knew it would give him the financial security he needed and us the finest-looking films.

Anyhow, no sooner had I returned to London than Lewis Gilbert called me at home, and asked if I could fly to Bogotá. He had a problem with his Line Producer, Victor Linden, and wanted to remove him from the picture. Of course Lewis didn't want to be the man who fired anyone, so I flew out and took Victor to one side. I said I was sorry it wasn't going to work out, and he left. We then had to re-organise things and bring in another Line Producer.

Meanwhile, Lewis' wife Hylda was accused of stealing jewellery from the shop in the hotel they were staying in and it was fast becoming a diplomatic incident. The one thing Lewis and Hylda hated above anything else was bad publicity, and the fact that they could have afforded to buy the hotel, let alone the jewellery shop, made it all quite ridiculous. They're also the most truly unlikely thieves.

Realising there was no other way out, I arranged to make a payment to the jeweller and pay him off so that we could finish shooting the picture.

About ten years later, I read that footballer Bobby Moore was accused of the same crime, and had been arrested in Bogotá. I tracked Lewis down to Paris, where he was making the Bond film *Moonraker* and told him that whilst I didn't know Bobby Moore from Adam, he was obviously being unfairly blamed in the same way Hylda was.

"Yes you're right," he said.

"I think you should make an announcement Lewis, you're a prominent person and people know who you are. We need to expose this."

Within the hour, Lewis called back and said Hylda thought it wasn't a good idea to bring it all up, as it made her look bad and fingers might be pointed. He said he'd rather let the whole thing drop. I asked if he thought I, as Head of Production at Warner Bros. (as I was then), should make a statement.

"I'd rather you didn't," he replied. So, regrettably, I let it drop.

Back to Bogatá and *The Adventurers*, and having sorted out the problems I received a call from Charlie Bluhdorn to fly to Wengen in Switzerland to fix another film. Having duly landed in Wengen, wearing a light linen suit - the only outfit I thought I'd need in Bogatá - my first port of call was to a clothes shop to buy a thick winter coat and warm clothes. I didn't even have a suitcase to live out of!

But all of my adventures and travels for Paramount fade into insignificance against the nightmare that was *Darling Lili,* which started out life in 1968. It was an American musical set in WWI, a sort of spin on the Mata

Darling Lili
PARAMOUNT PRESENTE
UNE PRODUCTION BLAKE EDWARDS
avec
JULIE ANDREWS · ROCK HUDSON
dans
DARLING LILI
et avec
JEREMY KEMP
TECHNICOLOR (R) PANAVISION (R)
LANCE PERCIVAL
MICHAEL WITNEY
JACQUES MARIN
ANDRE MARANNE
GLORIA PAUL
PRODUIT ET REALISE PAR BLAKE EDWARDS
PRODUCTEUR EXECUTIF OWEN CRUMP
ECRIT PAR BLAKE EDWARDS et WILLIAM PETER BLATTY
NOUVELLES CHANSONS DE JOHNNY MERCER et HENRY MANC
MUSIQUE DIRIGEE PAR HENRY MANCINI
NUMEROS MUSICAUX MIS EN SCENE PAR HERMES PAN

Hari story, co-written and directed by Blake Edwards, and starring Julie Andrews with Rock Hudson.

Originally to be based out of Paris (as was *The Adventurers*), the French riots of the late 1960s - which started with a series of student protests against capitalism, consumerism and traditional institutions, spread like lightning to factories involving more than 20% of the total population of France and at the time presented such a fear of civil uprising that President DeGaulle left Paris for two days - and so our film understandably relocated partly to Brussels for a short period and then on to Ireland.

I must preface what I'm about to write with the somewhat amusing statement on a well known internet reference site which states, "Blake Edwards suffered continual interference from Paramount Pictures executives while making the film".

I, unfortunately, was one of those executives.

However in reality it was a film I had no input on whatsoever in terms of budget, schedule or anything else. It arrived on these shores from LA and I pretty much inherited everything that had been prepared there as a *fait accompli.*

Within a few weeks the film was running miles behind schedule, and was heading towards being millions over budget. It was, as you might have gathered from my brief plot synopsis, not what you would call an overly commercial story, and so it going over budget so soon in the process was seriously bad news. (In the event it cost $25 million and recouped just $5m on its US release.)

I received a call from Bluhdorn who told me he was flying into Dublin at the weekend and he wanted to meet me there at the Gresham Hotel. No sooner had we both met in the Irish capital than Charlie said, "Let's go out to the set."

We arrived on location, on what was one of the most beautiful days with blue skies and bright sunshine, to find all the crew playing around in front of the WWI planes with Frisbees - then the new craze. I said to the production manager that Mr. Bluhdorn wanted to see Blake.

"Oh, he's having a massage."

**Julie Andrews and Blake Edwards**

"Would you tell him that Mr. Bluhdorn, the owner of Paramount, is here?" I asked. I'd already warned the production office that we were coming over, so was less than impressed by this reception.

"When he's finished his massage he'll be with you," was the response.

Eventually Blake came out, and I could sense the atmosphere on set was pretty terrible, so asked him, "Why aren't we filming?"

"Hey man, how can we film on a day like this?" he replied. "Have you ever seen aeroplanes in a sky without any clouds? There's no way I can shoot today unless some clouds appear."

"Well, isn't there anything else you could film?" I asked.

"I was prepared for, and rehearsed to do, the stuff in the sky."

I was pleased Charlie was there to see first-hand what was happening, and to maybe get an idea of what my job often entailed. This was a rather unique working experience with Blake though, as he would never discuss anything - he just knew he was right.

It was a pretty fruitless visit, and so we left.

A few weeks later, with everything running even more over budget, we had another meeting with Blake and this time Julie Andrews was there too, and - yet again - with nothing resolved we then had a separate, private meeting with just Julie. Charlie said he wanted to change director, which was perhaps not the most tactful thing to say to her at that moment as although they weren't yet married, it was very much on the cards she and Edwards would be soon.

"Well get me a list of directors," she replied.

Charlie produced a list of some of the biggest and hottest directors working in the business, and Julie said, as she took the list from Charlie, "You know I have approval of director?"

"Yes we do," he said.

After a cursory look she said, "Well I don't approve anybody on this list. The only director I approve is Blake."

That was the end of the conversation.

Everything carried on and after they moved locations, Bluhdorn flew out again to meet with them in a further attempt to rein things in. This time though, to perhaps deflect what they saw as further interference, Blake and Julie brought their children to the meeting; which really gives you an insight as to where it was all heading!

Someone once said of producer Sam Goldwyn, "You know where you're going with him - nowhere!" That's where we were with Blake.

Day by day afterwards Charlie would scream down the phone to me, "Are we still over budget?" and of course we were, so in a last-ditch attempt to try and restore things Charlie decided to appoint my old friend John Dark to the production to oversee things on a daily basis.

John, after figuring things out, met with me and we told Charlie, "You're not going to achieve anything different with John on board as Blake will still be in charge and running the schedule. Julie won't back anyone else's decisions but Blake's."

John's hands would have been tied from day one and he wouldn't have been able to take the decisions he needed to.

Blake was determined this film would help undo the typecasting of Julie Andrews as a sweet, sugary character into a sexy screen seductress, and with their romance blossoming I think he was blinkered to the realities of the situation.

Afterwards he blamed Paramount for insisting that he filmed in Ireland and said, "It's not just that there isn't much sunshine there, you can shoot a movie in consistent bad weather, but you can't count on that in Ireland, either. There are days when either it's pissing rain or you get intermittent sun; for the most part, Ireland's just a bad place to shoot a movie. I investigated that immediately and wanted to shoot the aircraft sequences in South Carolina, which can be made to look like German or French countryside, but Paramount stuck to its decision to shoot in Ireland, so off we went. Well, the second unit ran millions of dollars over budget just waiting to get 'clear air' shots there. After that, I was under constant money pressure from the studio but that wasn't nearly as hard to take as the rest of the stuff they did to me."

Edwards continued, in his attempt to blame everyone else: "the film was a product of people taking over a motion-picture company without having any credentials at all. By that, I mean Charlie Bluhdorn giving directives and Bob [Robert] Evans, who'd hardly made a movie before, being head of the studio."

I took exception to what Blake said, as I was there on the ground and knew different. I might add that Bob Evans turned the studio around from being the ninth to the most successful US studio during his tenure.

Of course, had the film been a runaway success instead of a critically indifferent one, I'm sure Blake would have happily taken all the credit and lauded Bob Evans, but on its release the film fared badly at the box office. Some critics questioned why a musical version of Mata Hari had been greenlit in the first place, but for a certain budget with the right team, I feel it could have been an interesting project. It just all ran away with itself.

It was eventually released on VHS, but rates as one of Blake Edwards' lesser seen and known movies; he went on to make the more successful *S.O.B.* which was really a film based around the making of *Darling Lili.*

***The Italian Job***

My time at Paramount didn't involve only problem movies, there were many joyful ones too - *The Italian Job* (1969) being one. It was pitched by a young producer named Michael Deeley, who had this script about a daring robbery in Italy, in Minis. Michael ran the show very well, and pulled together a terrific cast headed by Michael Caine; the only time I was called in was when they wanted to get rid of their production manager, René Dupont, and bring in someone else, so of course I was the man charged with that job!

The film did very good business in the UK, though in the US it didn't do as well and I know Michael Caine has said he believes it was down to an ill-judged marketing campaign, showing the lead characters with guns on the posters. It wasn't a gangster movie of course.

*Monte Carlo Or Bust* (1969) was another happy production, from director Ken Annakin, and it boasted an all-star cast including Tony Curtis,

Susan Hampshire, Terry-Thomas and Dudley Moore to name but a few, was a British-French-Italian co-production costing Paramount just $10m, and made a terrific return - which further hammers a nail in the coffin of *Darling Lili* as far as I'm concerned.

*Barbarella* (1968) was a film on which I learned a valuable sales lesson.

It was a film I pretty much inherited again, and was a French-Italian production with Roger Vadim directing his then wife Jane Fonda, in a rather bizarre sci-fi story. At the first screening, Charles Bluhdorn said he didn't think it was very good, but obviously saw something in it, as he said he wanted to release it worldwide on the same day.

"We'll do a big publicity campaign!" he declared.

They ran clips on TV of Jane Fonda and David Hemmings, in the most fantastic costumes, and they were making love by just touching fingers. It was actually quite erotic, and Bluhdorn knew it would attract huge crowds to the opening weekend.

"When they come out and say 'that wasn't very good' it doesn't matter as they've all bought their tickets," he said.

It was a very intelligent move on Bluhdorn's part as it avoided negative publicity having a damaging impact on the release, and although it didn't do spectacular business at the box office it has since become a cult movie and is rumoured to be in the process of being remade.

A lot of the films I was involved with were Italian co-productions, and I think it was largely due to Charlie loving Italy and because of him and producer Dino DeLaurentiis being so close. Dino produced *Barbarella* too.

One Saturday evening I was having dinner with Charlie - it was just the two of us - in Rome and he said he'd forgotten it was his wife's birthday the next day. "Could you get hold of Dino? Ask him to phone Bulgari and have them open up tomorrow morning at 11am?" he said.

This was in the days long before mobile phones, so I tracked down Dino's secretary, who in turn called Dino.

On the way to the airport the next morning, Charlie and I stopped off at Bulgari's magnificent jewellery store and he bought a necklace for his wife; he said,

PARAMOUNT PICTURES presents
A DINO DE LAURENTIIS PRODUCTION
JANE FONDA
The space age adventuress whose sex-ploits are among the most bizarre ever seen.
SEE
BARBARELLA
DO HER THING!
STARRING
JOHN PHILLIP LAW · MARCEL MARCEAU
DAVID HEMMINGS
UGO TOGNAZZI
DINO DE LAURENTIIS · ROGER VADIM
Lyrics and Music by Bob Crewe and Charles Fox · Performed by The Bob Crewe Generation Orchestra Available on Dynavoice Records
SCREENPLAY BY TERRY SOUTHERN
A FRANCO-ITALIAN CO-PRODUCTION · DINO DE LAURENTIIS · CINEMATOGRAFICA S.p.A. · MARIANNE PRODUCTIONS · PANAVISION® TECHNICOLOR®
SUGGESTED FOR MATURE AUDIENCES

"Paul, is there anything here you'd like, because we're going to get a discount?"

I couldn't afford the box the jewels were in, let alone anything else! But Charlie's world was a different one to everyone else's.

I remember on one occasion Charlie and Martin Davis had been granted an audience with the Pope, and I got a message a day or two before from Charlie asking if he could reschedule from Wednesday to Thursday. I said he had to be joking, it was difficult enough getting in to see the Pope as it was, and it wasn't like meeting an actor saying, "Could you come tomorrow instead of today". But Charlie lived in his own little world and was used to being told "yes" to everything he asked.

When the director Lindsay Anderson was setting up a film with Paramount, his production manager Roy Baird came in to see me.

"Paul, we're going to do this film called *If*," he explained.

"If what?" I asked.

"No, it's called *IF*. Lindsay is going to do it and he's speaking to Bluhdorn tonight."

Sure enough, a decision was made on the phone and what Bluhdorn said, went. It was the same with *Oh! What A Lovely War* (1969); Richard Attenborough spoke to Charlie, and it was all agreed. I knew Dick of old, from my Rank days, and my having that friendship and knowing him was a huge help in my position as with it being Dick's first film as director, with him having replaced John Mills, many would have been unsure about his request to have Kevin Connor as his editor - Kevin was a very good assistant editor, but a first time editor with a first time director could be a risk too far. However Dick was someone who was always confident in his decisions, and he would never gamble on someone he wasn't 100% confident in.

"If this film goes wrong I'll have Charlie on my back," I kept thinking to myself, but Dick assured me he felt Kevin was the best man for the job and wanted me to support him in the decision. We never had any problems at all,

THE MUSICAL SHOT IN THE ARM!
THE EVER POPULAR WAR GAMES WITH SONGS BATTLES & A FEW JOKES
PARAMOUNT PICTURES PRESENTS AN ACCORD PRODUCTION
OH! WHAT A LOVELY WAR
GUEST STARS (IN ALPHABETICAL ORDER)
DIRK BOGARDE PHYLLIS CALVERT JEAN PIERRE CASSEL JOHN CLEMENTS JOHN GIELGUD JACK HAWKINS KENNETH MORE
LAURENCE OLIVIER MICHAEL REDGRAVE VANESSA REDGRAVE RALPH RICHARDSON MAGGIE SMITH SUSANNAH YORK JOHN MILLS
AS SIR DOUGLAS HAIG
PRODUCED BY BRIAN DUFFY and RICHARD ATTENBOROUGH
DIRECTED BY RICHARD ATTENBOROUGH
G
PANAVISION® COLOR A PARAMOUNT PICTURE
69/306

and Kevin went on to edit Dick's next film and became a successful director in his own right.

I will say that Charlie Bluhdorn was someone who would support me emphatically. He loved the deal, he loved meeting actors and sitting to chat with them, but he was never interested in getting more involved in productions. He made decisions and moved on - and sometimes they weren't necessarily the right decisions, as with *Inadmissible Evidence* in 1968. Charlie thought the legal drama sounded quite prestigious, as after all it was based on a John Osborne play.

Osborne adapted the script but it really was very 'stagey' in feel. There were plot holes and confusing points that were never fully explained. So much so, it never saw the light of day when completed. I remember sitting in a first screening, and as with many other Paramount films, the director or producer were there. They were desperately keen to hear what Charlie thought, but he would turn to me after the lights went up and say, "What do you think, Hitchcock?" I'd always be the first to have to speak, which of course wasn't what the filmmakers wanted.

It was always a little tricky with Charlie because, naturally, he wanted to be everyone's friend and never deliver bad news - at least not personally!

Another of the projects Charlie felt was a winner, but I thought otherwise, was *The Bliss Of Mrs Blossom* (1968) - and I don't think it's been seen since it was first released either.

It was made in Twickenham, and Charlie liked the idea when it was pitched, of having Dickie Attenborough and Shirley McLain in a film, and with James Booth too, that really sealed it. The story was all about Harriet Blossom (McLain) having a repairman (Booth) come in from her husband's (Attenborough) bra factory to fix her sewing machine, and she had a fling with him and moved him into the attic as her lover. It was supposed to be a comedy, but raised few laughs and did little for anyone's career nor for the Paramount coffers I'm afraid.

Then there was *Waterloo* (1970), a film Dino De Laurentiis brought to us, but one Charlie didn't really want to make after the promised starring of

Peter O'Toole changed to Rod Steiger; it caused a lot of headaches and difficult meetings, resulting in Paramount only taking domestic (USA) rights - and that was out of friendship to Dino really.

Oh, we also green-lit a picture with Basil Dearden, called *The Assassination Bureau* (1969); we were the first western film company to go to Prague – and before the Russian invasion of 1968 - so when I was asked, "Have you ever worked in Prague before?" it was a completely irrelevant question as it happens, as every film is different regardless of where it shoots. We found some good people, got on with it and finished on schedule. Bud Ornstein was the one who pushed that project through, and again Charlie wasn't very interested as he didn't feel the cast was big enough. Charlie wanted stars, big pictures and prestige!

Needless to say, when Barbra Streisand and director Vincent Minelli teamed up to make *On A Clear Day* (1970), Charlie was all for it. Part of it was filmed in Brighton on the south coast, so I was assigned to that section of the production and found Minelli to be extremely creative, if a little 'strange'. I got on very well with Barbra though and when *Yentl* (released in 1983) came along some years later (at Warner Bros.) I was involved to a much greater extent. I remember we set off for Prague with production designer Roy Walker to open up the office, and on a daily basis travelled around with Barbra looking for locations.

The interesting thing was she'd already agreed the look of her character, and the costumes she'd wear in each scene; so when we scouted for possible locations she brought the said costumes with her, would go into a local bar or hotel to get changed into them and have some Polaroids taken to see what she looked like.

We then all flew to LA for meetings, and it was an absolute pleasure working with Barbra but I'm afraid we suffered quite a lot of interference from Warner's, who were nervous about the star also directing. There was some sort of co-production deal with Orion pictures, and when United Artists went bust in 1981 due to *Heaven's Gate* (1980) bankrupting the studio, Orion cancelled all films with a budget of over $14 million.

Barbra was determined to make the film, and asked me to stay with her full-time, but my Warner's contract precluded that. Eventually MGM financed the movie in 1982.

*Half A Sixpence* (1967) had been a very successful stage musical, which was based on an H. G. Wells novel and follows the story of a draper's assistant falling in love with a chambermaid, and how he comes into and loses a fortune but finds the most valuable thing he has is true love.

Charlie Bluhdorn really liked the musical, so when the idea of a film was brought to him, he readily backed it.

Tommy Steele reprised the lead role, and American director George Sidney was engaged to helm the movie at Shepperton Studios. George was one of the most respected and experienced of directors, having made a lot of Hollywood musicals such as *Kiss Me Kate, Pal Joey, Viva Las Vegas* etc. and Gillian Lynne was brought in to choreograph (she later worked on most of Lloyd-Webber's West End musicals). There were a lot of production problems relating to the look of the film and, in turn, the budget. In fairness it wasn't easy for Sidney as he was working in an entirely different atmosphere to that he'd been used to in LA, and he'd worked with the greats such as Frank Sinatra, Rita Hayworth, Elvis Presley and Kim Novak; in fact he summed up his feeling to me at lunch one day by saying, "England is the home of the professional amateur."

Bluhdorn appointed John Dark to join as Executive Producer to help get things back on track, and when completed we ran a preview of the film - the results were not good.

One of the numbers in the stage musical - *Crash Bang Wallop* - had been left out as the film looked set to over-run (in fact it came in at 2 hours 20 in the end), but it was felt the famous song needed to be included so we set up at Elstree Studios (as Shepperton was fully booked), filmed the extra scene, and added it into the final cut. Alas, though it helped a little, it was not enough to make the film a box office success.

YUL BRYNNER
ROBERT MITCHUM
VILLA CABALGA
CON GRAZIA BUCCELLA · HERBERT LOM · ROBERT VIHARO Y CHARLES BRONSON
ESCRITA POR ROBERT TOWNE Y SAM PECKINPAH • ADAPTADA POR WILLIAM DOUGLAS LANSFORD
BASADA EN LA NOVELA "PANCHO VILLA" DE WILLIAM DOUGLAS LANSFORD • PRODUCIDA POR TED RICHMOND • DIRECTOR BUZZ KULIK
MUSICA DE MAURICE JARRE
TECHNICOLOR
PANAVISION
PARAMOUNT PICTURE

*Villa Rides* shot in Madrid in 1968 with Yul Brynner, Robert Mitchum and Charles Brosnan. It was a very good cast and no doubt appealed to Charlie hugely.

One day Charlie rang me and said, "Paul, would you meet me in Madrid on Tuesday? Brynner wants to talk to me about something. We'll go to the set and have lunch with him."

I duly met Charlie at the Hilton in Madrid, drove to the set with him and we parked up outside Brynner's huge, huge trailer. He was a little guy with a huge ego!

We had lunch, all served by waiters silver service style, and at the end Brynner looked at me and said, "Paul, would you mind leaving Charlie and me alone as I need to talk to him."

"Fine. I'll see you back on the set."

I was walking back when I bumped into Robert Mitchum, who was returning from the catering tent - I'd actually got to know him from another film we'd made in Kenya, and he said, "What are you doing here, Hitch?"

"I came out with Bluhdorn for lunch with Brynner. I don't know why you don't live like that," I said, gesturing at the trailer behind me. "We've just had chateaubriand, the Chateau Neuf du Pape wine..."

"You know why I don't?" asked Mitchum. "Because I can fucking act!"

I've never forgotten that line.

Back on set they started shooting, though the director Buzz Kulik made it clear he didn't like me being around as he thought I was there to spy on him; but the film was all on budget and schedule so it never worried me.

After a short while Charlie appeared and said he was ready to go. "What was all that about?" I asked.

"Oh, Brynner wanted to talk about a film he wants to make, but we won't be doing it."

Charlie always was very approachable for stars and would often drop everything to meet them, and often waste time and money doing so. But such was his character.

Robert Evans ran the overall production side of Paramount and he became every big star's friend, and green-lit many successful films including *The Odd Couple, Rosemary's Baby, True Grit* and *The Godfather* to name but a few. Charlie - his direct boss, as he was mine - meanwhile, was always much more interested in European films and co-productions and added more and more to our slate; however, along with the increased activity came increased pressure and workloads. I realised my life wasn't my own any longer; I was like a travelling salesman dispatched here, there and everywhere at a moment's notice and every time the phone rang, I never knew what it'd be about or where I'd have to shoot off to.

I started getting the most terrible debilitating headaches, and became very ill, so much so I convinced myself I had a brain tumour. My local doctor - who was a family friend actually, and could see what my job was like - was convinced I was suffering the effects of stress, but nevertheless arranged for me to go for a private scan, which was all pretty new technology back then, and quite expensive.

Afterwards he came to the house and (happily) said, "You've just wasted £500 Paul, the results are clear. Your problem is tension." He told me I needed a total break.

I'd never had a proper holiday in three years and whilst my wife never said I should give the job up, I hardly ever saw her or my children for any length of time and I was missing out.

These were the deciding factors in my tendering my resignation to Bluhdorn.

Looking back, I guess I must have been responsible for nearly 100 films in three years, and despite bringing in a guy to help me look after the foreign co-productions, I was hands-on each and every day. I like to think I carried out my duties to the very best of my abilities, and always served the interests of the company first. Charlie didn't share my view though; he wasn't very complimentary when he received my letter, and certainly didn't thank me for doing a good job.

I guess he thought he 'owned' me and that I'd stay with him forever. He honestly believed I was being terribly ungrateful and said as much in a rather unpleasant letter, which also inferred I'd find it very difficult to get another job.

I kept that letter for a very long time, as to be honest it hurt me deeply.

But work was the last thing on my mind. I was burned out and needed to re-charge my batteries.

# 1969

## *Joining Warner Bros.*

A few weeks after quitting Paramount I was able, for the first time in years, to join my family on a summer holiday in Spain. I'd only ever managed a long weekend, at best, before and this was such a treat and hugely relaxing - I felt a great weight had been lifted off my shoulders.

However, mid-way through it I received a message to call Bud Ornstein. I wondered what it could be about; he'd certainly have heard I'd left Paramount, but I wasn't interested in rushing into another job before I'd had a nice long break. Nevertheless, I called him.

"What are you doing?" he asked.

"I'm on holiday Bud, in Marbella."

"When I retire I'm going to buy a place down there," he said. I know Bud had received some sort of award for services to the Spanish film industry so was very familiar with the area, and whilst it was nice to talk a little about the sights and sounds of Marbella, Bud soon cut to the chase with, "What are you going to do afterwards?"

"I don't know Bud, I'll have to think about finding a job at some point I suppose."

"I've just been offered the chance of running a major studio in the States. Would you be interested in joining me?"

"Who is it with Bud, and when?" I asked reticently.

"We'd have to fly out to LA on Sunday (it was Tuesday when we spoke) and I'll introduce you. If we all get on and like one another we'll take it from there."

I was minded to say "no" but then thought about the mortgage, the children and the fact I had absolutely nothing else on the horizon, and whilst I wasn't keen to rush into another studio role, let's just say he'd grabbed my attention enough to be intrigued.

"They'll pay all our expenses, but I've been sworn to secrecy as to who it is as the company is about to be bought out."

A few days later I was back in London, preparing for another trip to California!

Bud booked us seats in first class and as soon as we took off I leaned across and said, "So Bud, who are we going to meet?"

"A guy called Steve Ross has bought out Kenneth Hyman's interests in Warner Bros-Seven Arts," he explained.

Ken Hyman, I should explain, is a film producer perhaps best known for *The Dirty Dozen*. In 1967 he paid Jack Warner $32 million for his shares in Warner Bros. and merged his Seven Arts Productions with it. In the next couple of years they made over 30 films, including hits like *Bullitt, Cool Hand Luke, The Green Berets, The Wild Bunch* and a few films with Hammer including *Dracula Has Risen From The Grave.*

In 1969, Steve Ross' company Kinney National which owned everything from rental cars, parking companies to DC comics, a wood flooring manufacturer and - I seem to remember - funeral parlours, bought out Ken Hyman's interests.

"It will become Warner Bros. again; it will be the resurrection of the studio," Bud explained.

We again stayed with Aunty Mary Pickford, who was still in bed. I of course had three years worth of stories to share with her!

We had our meetings, they seemed to like me, and offered me the job as Head of Production outside the US.

They suggested I head back to London and reorganise the Warner's office there, which was on Berkeley Square. I asked who was in the office, but they didn't know.

"Ken's out, so go and see who is there and change anyone you want," they said.

I flew home on the Saturday, and the following Monday I collected my paperwork and travelled up to Berkeley Square. I knocked on the door and the receptionist asked how she could help.

"My name is Paul Hitchcock," I said rather proudly.

"Yes, and? Are you here to see someone?" she asked.

"Who is here?"

"The head of production is Ray Anzarut," she replied.

"Is he in?"

"Yes, he's in his office."

"Well would you mind telling him I'm here?" I asked.

I was stumbling, and feeling like a bit of a Charlie.

"There's a man here named Paul Hitchcock," she said on the phone. Obviously, being a production person, Ray knew my name but the receptionist looked up and said, "He can't see you without an appointment. You'll have to come back at 2.30pm."

It was then around 10.30am and I had been sent to take over an office that I couldn't get into!

With my briefcase in hand I walked over to the Paramount office, where I knew most of the staff, and of course they thought they'd never see me again; so when I told them my story and asked if I could sit somewhere to read my newspaper for a few hours they all fell about laughing.

At 2.30pm I returned to the Berkeley Square office and met Ray.

"What can I do for you?" he asked.

"Has Kenny Hyman not told you?"

"What's Kenny Hyman got to do with it?"

"He no longer owns the company," I explained, "and I have now been appointed Head of Production."

"Well I've heard nothing about it and you're certainly not coming into these offices until I've had it confirmed," he said.

"I suggest you make some calls tonight," I replied and left. I guess if I had been in his position I wouldn't have been very pleasant either.

I returned home and called Bud in the USA.

"How's it gone?" he asked.

"How's it gone," I laughed, "I couldn't get in the office until 2.30pm and was out within fifteen minutes. They're all in situ there and know nothing about the changes."

"I don't believe it. I'll make some calls."

A couple of hours later Bud phoned back and said that they'd all been told and I was to go in to the office the next morning to take things over.

A short while afterwards Bud arrived to check out the offices, which were really quite small and plain, and he didn't like that at all - he wanted something more prestigious. So we moved and rented three floors in a more imposing building on nearby Cork Street.

Within a month of taking over, I was told Warner's were keen to make *Out Of Africa* with Liv Ullman, to be directed by Tony Harvey. I headed off on a recce to look at all the locations, in Africa, and afterwards when I landed back in London I thought I'd best report to Bud.

"Bud's no longer here," I was told.

"He's left?! Here we go again, take two..."

It seemed Bud had wanted to make different films to the ones Warner's were proposing, and so he quit.

Ted Ashley - a former talent agent - was running the show in Burbank as CEO and Chairman, and reported directly to Steve Ross, but I didn't really know him and certainly didn't enjoy the sort of relationship I had with Bud (or Charlie Bluhdorn before, for that matter), so was worried that I too would be out on my ear.

Fortunately, over the coming months it all seemed to work out and I stayed on in my position, and when Frank Wells (who headed up the production division) arrived in London for some meetings, we got together and got along well. Frank asked me if I had any thoughts or ideas about the London office, and if we might improve anything.

"Actually, yes," I suggested, "we're paying a lot of money to be at this address, and with cleaning, security and parking costs added in it all mounts up. If we were based at a studio such as Pinewood, all that is part of the package and I think would be more cost effective."

Given that I was spending a lot of time at Pinewood on productions in any event, it made sense to me to relocate there.

"Do an exercise," Frank replied - he was a man of few words. "Give me the pros and cons."

I spoke to studio Managing Director Cyril Howard, who in turn suggested that they might build us a US-style studio bungalow in the grounds. He estimated the cost to be something like £90,000 and in return asked if we would give him a three-year commitment to base ourselves at the studio. The numbers added up to a 40% saving, and I knew meeting with executives and filmmakers at Pinewood would be far easier (and more attractive) than in an office in the West End. Warner's stayed at Pinewood for three decades as it happens.

"Ok, move on," Frank said. He didn't talk about it for days, or fire off memos for other people to comment on, he made decisions.

Whilst the new Pinewood bungalow was being built we located to another building at the studio and I brought out our Business Affairs Executive, my PA, and a story editor - it was a small, tight-knit team. I didn't need anyone else because I knew I would appoint the right people to make our movies, and accordingly wouldn't need to continually check up on them. I'd speak to the production manager at the end of each day, or of course they'd call me if there was a problem they needed to discuss; I'm not talking about all the nitty-gritty details, but if they were due to start filming at 9am and didn't get underway until 1pm because of some issue, that's what I needed to know about.

In all the years I looked after Warner's, I ran things on trust; I established relationships with the directors and producers, but was always there to support them, and they in turn trusted me.

Bud Ornstein told me he'd proposed resurrecting a film called *Performance* to the studio executives. It starred Mick Jagger, James Fox and Anita Pallenberg. It had been green-lit under the previous management regime, but when they viewed a first cut Kenneth Hyman & Co. felt the dark, experimental film was just about as far removed from what they thought would be an equivalent to The Beatles' *A Hard Day's Night*, than anything else imaginable. Scenes of gratuitous violence, sex and drug-taking led to calls for the negative to be destroyed.

With footage literally sitting on a shelf, I was then asked by Bud to calculate how much it would cost to resurrect the film, re-cut it and get some sort of release. They felt there was some commercial merit in the casting, though I think the end result made the executives feel they should have left it on the shelf as it was pretty much vilified by the critics and was totally uncommercial!

Nowadays the film has been rediscovered and reappraised by audiences and it's regarded as something of a cult.

The Devils, directed by Ken Russell

# 1970

## *The Devils*

Directed by Ken Russell and starring Oliver Reed and Vanessa Redgrave, *The Devils* is one of the most controversial films I've been involved with, in terms of its subject matter - it's an historical account of the rise and fall of Urbain Grandier, a 17th-century Roman Catholic priest executed for witchcraft following supposed possessions in France. Oliver Reed played Grandier and Vanessa Redgrave played a sexually-repressed nun who found herself, albeit inadvertently, responsible for the accusations.

The film shot at Pinewood and on locations in the UK, and having been on set for some of the filming I made it a point to go first thing every day across to Denham Laboratories to see the previous day's rushes. I was just grateful I never had any breakfast beforehand as what I saw on the screen was pretty unpalatable to put it mildly. The highly controversial commentary on religion was certain to stir controversy but that combined with graphic violence and disturbing sexual content, well, I just knew we'd be lucky to get an 'X' certificate: leaving aside disturbing exorcisms, there was language such as "cunt" and "fuck me" and a whole two-and-a-half-minute sequence of crazed naked nuns sexually assaulting a statue of Christ! Then there was another scene of Sister Jeanne (Redgrave) masturbating with a charred leg bone of Grandier at the end of the film. It was just too much.

During post-production the Warner executives tried to get the director to agree to making cuts, but of course he stood his ground and refused. It eventually became a game of compromise between Russell, the executives and the censors. In the event, to be granted an 'X' certificate in the UK, Russell agreed to cut down scenes with explicit nudity and unacceptable language, but Warner's then removed (without the director's consent) much of the aforementioned masturbation scene, and the whole of the crazed nuns sequence. I know even more was cut for the US release, but without those cuts, it would have been impossible to screen the film - this was 1970/71 remember, and values and tastes were very much different to those of today.

However, despite these cuts a great many local authorities in the UK still banned cinemas in their area from showing the movie, and the full version has been denied a video and DVD release to this day. It was not a box office success and subsequent requests from the directors to restore the 'missing footage' were turned down by Warner's, though it has seemingly found a cult audience with some critics now saying it was one of Russell's best films.

## *A Clockwork Orange (1970 -1971)*

Stanley Kubrick was hailed unlike any other director at Warner Bros.

He had complete control over script, casting, production, editing and the final negative. That was a given on any project he started. Quite often, no one at the studio would see a script - they just agreed to back his next movie.

After *2001: A Space Odyssey*, Kubrick had planned to make a film about Napoleon Bonaparte, but during pre-production Dino De Laurentiis' *Waterloo* was released and bombed at the box office, so instead he turned his attention to *A Clockwork Orange*. It was, and is, a disturbing, violent film centred on delinquency, gangs, social, political, and economic unrest in a dystopian Britain.

Malcolm McDowell was cast in the lead role and the film shot in and around London.

I'd of course heard of Kubrick but never met him in the flesh until film-

ing was underway on *Clockwork* and I visited the location one day. He was very reclusive and quite introverted; there was no warm welcome from him or a handshake that's for sure.

He'd previously phoned my office and asked me to negotiate a deal on an apartment he wanted to film in, for Malcolm McDowell's character, in Borehamwood. I'll never forget the flat; it was on the third floor, with no lift. Immediately the practicalities of getting cameras, lights and other equipment up there struck me, but that was the flat Stanley wanted. I did a deal with the couple who owned it to move out for a year. In fact it was over two years before they returned, living quite comfortably in a hotel in the meantime on the Warner's expense account.

The most ludicrous thing was that the windows were blacked out throughout the shoot. We could have been anywhere! But that was Stanley Kubrick for you - he wanted the "feeling" that they lived on the top floor.

I knew pretty much from then on that there was only one way we were going to make this film, and that was Stanley's way. Had I questioned, for instance, why we couldn't film in a ground floor apartment with windows blacked out, giving the crew much easier access, I know that would have marked the end of any association I might have had with Stanley; and no matter how shallow it might actually be, I knew I needed to maintain a working relationship with him, as Warner's were very keen to keep him as part of their family. I, on the other hand, was probably more dispensable!

I respected Stanley, and I'd like to think Stanley respected me. Whilst my loyalty was always to Warner Bros., I built a trust with Stanley insomuch as he knew I'd always keep my word to him and wouldn't interfere.

Incidentally the bulk of locations on any Kubrick film were, by and large, within a short drive of his north London home. Stanley was terribly travel-phobic and we used to joke that he needed his passport to go into London. He'd never fly anywhere; not even when he was trying to set up a film in Czechoslovakia, a WWII holocaust movie (which was shelved as soon as he heard Spielberg was starting *Schindler's List*). My assistant Lidia (who is now my second wife, I'm pleased to say) was doing some work with the production department out there, and I remember saying to her that Stanley working in Czechoslovakia was never going to happen; it was too far out of his comfort zone.

I digress.

**Warren Clarke (left) and Malcolm McDowell lead the cast**

One of my jobs was to try and estimate when one of his films would finish and how much it would cost. In fairness to Stanley, he'd always send us a cost statement for the week prior, but it was completely inaccurate. For instance he'd say it was an eight-week shooting schedule, and on week 6 of his cost reports he'd be showing us as being only one-third of the way through!

I knew it was ludicrous, as did the studio.

Terry Semel summed it up best one day when he said to me, "I love announcing the studio is about to make another Stanley Kubrick film, but I dread us starting!"

In all the years I worked with Stanley - and it was the best part of two decades - I never once saw a script. I'd occasionally see a few pages and would have a schedule with descriptive passages, but I never knew what the films were really about beyond that. The schedule by the way was always inaccurate as it wasn't based on any foundation – i.e. a completed script - and was really a best guesstimate. I know on *Clockwork* we shot four times the duration of the schedule I'd originally been given.

Nevertheless, I could roughly estimate where we were and how far we had to go in any one week, and would be able to say, for example, that the film

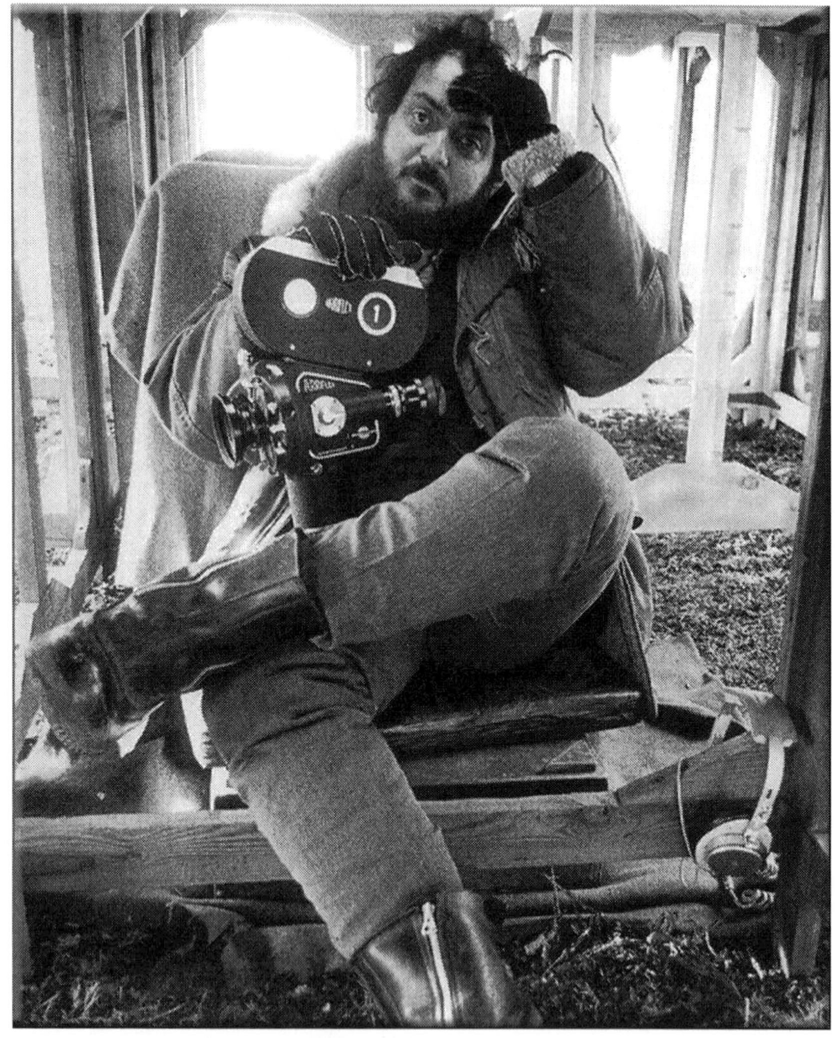

**Stanley Kubrick, on location**

they thought would cost $20 million would in fact be nearer to $60 million.

Stanley had a regular production manager named Bernard Williams, and Bernie was brilliant in 'handling' his boss; he anticipated what Stanley wanted and made sure everything worked. He would talk to me about what they were shooting that week, but would stop short of giving me any intricate information or detail as he knew if Stanley decided to change anything around then I might question it. This way I had an overall idea of what would be happening and the general requirements of the week, which Bernie knew would satisfy me and my bosses, but the in-between bits were their affair alone.

Bernie worked on the four Kubrick films I was involved with at Warner's and I respected him and his knowledge of running a picture greatly. So much so, when he asked that I visit the set one day during the filming of *Clockwork* because the crew were grumbling about the hours involved, Bernie said:

"We get in at 7am but it's after lunch before we start turning over the cameras, and we wrap at 9pm or even 10pm at night."

This was in the days when the several unions ACTT, NATKE, ETU etc. had huge influence over working hours and conditions, and were known to call strikes or "lights out" at a moment's notice, so I knew we had to tread carefully. I asked Bernie to gather the crew together, and I addressed them thus:

"Warner Brothers are not going to interfere in the way Stanley is making this movie. They are supporting him wholeheartedly, as I am, and Stanley is not going to change the way he works. This is not the army, this is moviemaking. If you want to make this film with Stanley, then we work by his rules; if you want to work on a conventional film that turns-over before 9am, breaks for lunch at 12.30 and wraps by 6pm then this is not it. If you'd rather leave, I'll understand, but if you'd like to stay then please be aware that Stanley sets the schedule."

Everybody appreciated my honesty, and all knuckled down without further word of mutiny thank goodness.

On every Kubrick movie we had a huge insurance claim which always resulted in a hiatus in production. This one was no exception; first Malcolm McDowell developed an eye infection and couldn't film, then something happened to some other actors ... and Stanley halted filming altogether.

The one thing with a Kubrick production was that Stanley owned all the equipment - the lights, cameras - and we'd still have to pay for them, or rather the insurers would, even if we weren't filming. One loss adjuster refused to continue paying for some of the equipment and Stanley reasoned, "But I'm losing revenue."

"Well rent it out," he replied.

**Stanley Kubrick in amongst the fast moving action**

"Rent it out!" Stanley exclaimed in horror.

Eventually, with a claim settled, production resumed.

I know his equipment wasn't the newest in the world, and indeed a bit of well-placed gaffer tape held parts of the cameras together on occasion, but he was certainly a shrewd businessman.

Stanley expected perfection in everything, and his version of perfection was not necessarily what we'd think was perfection! During post-production on *Clockwork* he phoned me at home one morning around 6am.

"Paul, are you a signatory to the Warner account?"

"Yes," I replied, "why?"

"Could you come over to me once you get yourself together?"

I had no idea what it was about, but said I would. Anyhow, I arrived at his house and he said he wanted me to follow him into London, to Humphreys Laboratories, and remove the negative of the movie because he'd noticed they'd damaged something.

So along with the editor, I had to drive to the lab and he took the negative to Denham Laboratories. Stanley's house, incidentally, had moviolas (editing machines) everywhere and really was like a mini-studio, though I never saw any footage until the first screening for the Warner Bros. executives in London's Soho Square many months later. There was a deathly silence in the room when the lights came up. Quite what the executives were expecting I'm not sure but Stanley had made them an extremely disturbing and violent film - a satirical science fiction theme of dealing with a youth culture where extreme violence has become 'normalised' and how the 'Establishment' cures such people especially with the use of things like aversion therapy to force a change in their ways. That very description is quite off-putting in itself but fortunately, as my involvement in the picture had now ended, I didn't have to pass comment nor see it again.

James Ferman, who was the film censor of the time, imposed an 'X' certificate, which meant no one under eighteen could see it at the cinema; of course that restricts the commercial prospects of any film quite severely.

Unfortunately, *A Clockwork Orange* was blamed for inciting several copycat crimes, including a fourteen-year-old boy who killed a classmate; and it was linked to the murder of an elderly vagrant by a sixteen-year-old boy in Bletchley, Buckinghamshire, who pleaded guilty after telling police that friends had told him of the film "and the beating up of an old boy like this one."

In the wake of all this negative press and the Kubrick family also receiving threats and having protesters outside their home, Stanley asked Warner Bros. to stop distribution in the UK.

"To try and fasten any responsibility on art as the cause of life seems to me to put the case the wrong way around," he said in a statement. "Art consists of reshaping life, but it does not create life, nor cause life. Furthermore, to attribute powerful suggestive qualities to a film is at odds with the scientifically accepted view that, even after deep hypnosis in a posthypnotic state, people cannot be made to do things which are at odds with their natures."

For the next twenty-seven years it was pretty near impossible to see the film. It was only after Stanley's passing in 1999 that the film was finally released on video and DVD. Needless to say, I never bought a copy.

# 1971

## *Man In The Wilderness*

Richard Sarafian directed this story of a group of 1800's fur trappers and Indian traders returning home with their goods, desperately attempting to beat the oncoming winter. When their guide Zachary Bass (Richard Harris) is injured in a bear attack, they decide to leave him behind to die. However he recovers, and swears revenge on them.

It wasn't actually a Warner Bros. film, but one which had been made independently and which the studio was interested in buying the distribution rights to. Deals had been agreed during production, but as shooting drew to an end in Almeria, Spain, producer Sandy Howard persuaded Warner's that they needed some extra cash to film a big action sequence, which everyone agreed would benefit the film.

I was asked to fly to Spain to ensure the additional budget was spent as agreed, and not elsewhere, and I must admit to enjoying my little sojourn in Soria, as one of the highlights was staying at the Parador Hotel, and having dinner most evenings with John Huston, who was co-starring. He regaled us with marvellous tales of his life and times, and those of his father actor Walter Huston.

By happy coincidence I discovered that I'd soon be working with John Huston again, not as an actor this time but as a director on *The Mackintosh Man.*

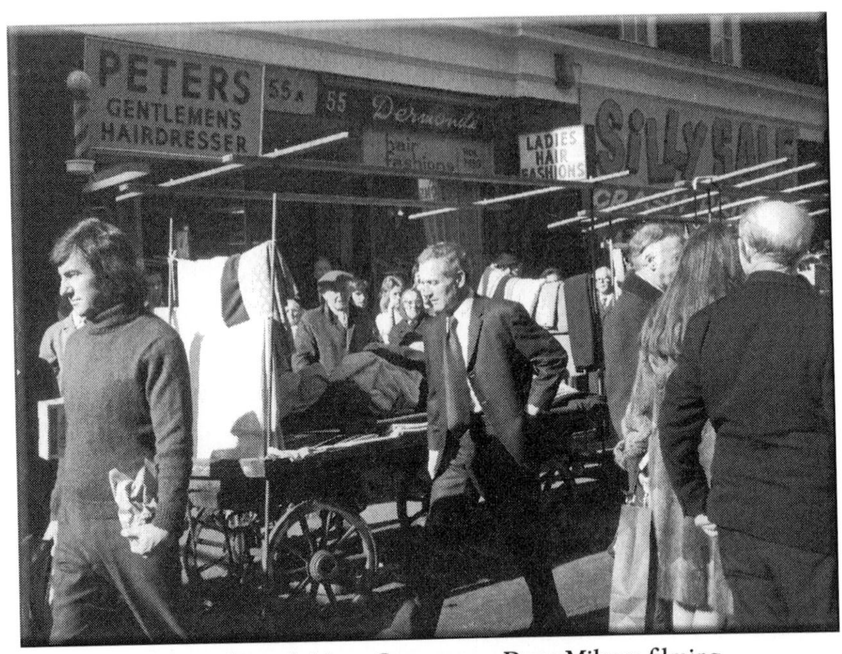


The Mackintosh Man - Cameraman Doug Milsom filming
Paul Newman in London loaction scenes

# 1973

## *The Mackintosh Man*

The film was based out of Pinewood, and directed by John Huston with Paul Newman starring. There were locations in the UK, Malta and Ireland too - which John always referred to as his ancestral homeland!

There never seemed to be a final script though, and during preparation we'd be handed different pages like confetti coming in, so it was a bit of a worry.

One day we went on a location recce in Ireland, and I travelled with Huston and Terry Marsh, our production designer. It was absolutely pouring with rain I remember; we pulled up outside a large building which Terry explained was going to be used for the interior of James Mason's character's office, and we should take a look.

Huston looked at the rain outside and said, "It's fine Terry, move on." It soon became apparent Mr. Huston was able to make instant, and correct, decisions.

In fact when Paul Newman wasn't involved in a scene, Huston was quite happy to leave the shot to his assistant Colin Brewer - he had faith in the very competent crew, and finished the film pretty much on schedule.

Our female lead was played by French actress Dominique Sanda, but unfortunately her accent was so heavy that she had to be re-voiced during post-production.

As mentioned James Mason was also in the film, and he played the villain 'Sir George Wheeler'. Early on in the prep period, his agent told us that Mason would only wear suits made by his personal tailor in Saville Row. Of course they were much more expensive than we had budgeted for, but so be it. After filming wrapped the same agent, Maggie Parker, called to say Mason wanted to buy the suits from us - for 30% of what we had paid. Given I'd told her, on several occasions, just how much the suits were costing us, I agreed that we'd accept 50%, especially as they'd hardly been worn. Mason refused to budge, so I donated the entire wardrobe to the local vicar who, in turn, passed them to his parishioners most in need of some clothing. Many months later the vicar called by my office at Pinewood to say just how grateful everyone had been.

This hadn't been the first time I'd encountered Mr Mason's demands!

## *Barry Lyndon (1973-1974)*

With the controversy and lack of commercial success of *A Clockwork Orange* on its original release, I felt Stanley Kubrick's next choice of subject was an unusual one, and, dare I say, uncommercial.

*Barry Lyndon* was announced by Warner's as being their next collaboration with their prized director.

Would you say a film based on the 1844 novel *The Luck of Barry Lyndon* by William Makepeace Thackeray, recounting the exploits of a fictional 18th-century Irish adventurer, was something audiences would rush to see?

The studio was obviously being somewhat cautious as to how it might recoup its budget, and were, as you can imagine, very keen to see the first footage available. However, unlike on any other film or with any other director, Stanley point-blank refused to let the studio bosses see any of the rushes that they'd paid for him to create! In fact The Daily Telegraph summed up the director-studio relationship rather succinctly by saying he was... "a perfectionist auteur who loomed larger over his movies than any concept or star." You might add "or any financier" too!

BARRY LYNDON
a film by
STANLEY KUBRICK
RYAN O'NEAL and
MARISA BERENSON
in BARRY LYNDON
with PATRICK MAGEE · HARDY KRUGER
DIANA KOERNER · GAY HAMILTON
Written for the screen, produced and directed by STANLEY KUBRICK
Based on the novel by WILLIAM MAKEPEACE THACKERAY
Music adapted and conducted by LEONARD ROSENMAN
Executive Producer JAN HARLAN
from Warner Bros. A Warner Communications Company
PG

Stanley engaged John Alcott as his cinematographer (he later won an Oscar for his work), and told John he wanted to film without using electric lighting for the many interior scenes and shoot by candlelight instead.

Shooting a film by candlelight?!

After experimenting with different combinations of lenses and film stock, Stanley got hold of three super-fast 50mm lenses which had been developed for use by NASA in the Apollo moon landings - where of course there were low light levels.

Principle photography was scheduled to take place in the Republic of Ireland, which doubled for locations in England and Prussia during the Seven Years' War. Ken Adam was the Production Designer and did a fantastic job, so everything looked great if nothing else - in fact Ken went on to win an Oscar for his work.

It must have been half-way through what was to be a 300-days' schedule when Stanley called me to say he'd been threatened by the IRA and wanted to leave Ireland immediately, but didn't want anyone else at Warner Bros. to know.

Bernie Williams arranged for him to travel by boat and then train to Salisbury in Wiltshire, travelling under the name of Bill Sykes (not the best pseudonym ever!) where a small team was assembled to complete the film. Mind you, Tony Waye, who was brought in as a production manager, walked off after a couple of weeks saying "Kubrick is a mad man." I wasn't overly surprised.

I never told Warner's about any of the relocation, and whenever they called asking about progress I'd say, "It's going fine."

It was only after Stanley was set up in Salisbury that I confessed to Terry Semel that they'd left Ireland, and reasoned I had to keep the confidence as otherwise I risked losing Stanley's trust and our working relationship.

Stanley was regarded as being quite mad within the industry, though latterly his brother-in-law Jan Harlan - who has become a self-appointed Kubrick spokesman - has only ever spoken of Stanley as being a creative genius. At no meeting I ever had with Kubrick either on the set, or with studio executives, was Harlan ever present, so it puzzles me how he can now be such an

**Marisa Berenson**

expert on what went on production-wise. He was primarily involved in the Kubrick family business and personal finances, but not in production. I feel it was only because he was Stanley's brother-in-law that he was "tolerated". Stanley would certainly have known about anything Harlan said or did. Julian Senior, the Warner head of publicity, will back me up in saying that prior to any premieres or first screenings, Stanley would call up and say something like, "I hear the cinema in Ecuador has a bulb in its second projector that's not at full capacity..."

He was all-seeing and all-knowing in every detail related to his films, to the point I really don't know how he found these things out. So he'd certainly have been fully aware of Harlan wanting to carve out a more important position for himself in production, but never rose to it. Now Stanley's no longer around, Harlan seems to have found his place as keeper of the empire.

There were delays and the obligatory insurance claim on *Barry Lyndon,* centring from the fact we had a problem with one of the lenses Stanley was using, and it turned out that the only other one in the world was at the NASA space centre! So that caused a delay in getting it shipped over.

The extra expense involved in the relocation and delays was difficult to accurately detail, but with production manager Bernie Williams I was able to estimate what each day would cost, say £100,000, and we added in forty days extra and then figured it would be an additional £4 million.

Stanley continued working and planning apace even when we weren't physically shooting, and I think it's fair to say he had no concept of time. He'd phone anybody he felt he needed to talk to, at 3am in the morning if need be, and think nothing of disturbing them. He often phoned me quite late at night and would be as sharp as a pin, whereas I was ready to fall into bed.

Another problem came when production designer Ken Adam was admitted to hospital suffering a nervous breakdown. Ken had worked with Stanley on *Dr. Strangelove* a decade earlier and in fact used to drive Stanley to Shepperton every day (at no more than 30 mph) so got to know him fairly well and the pair became very friendly.

"He saw himself as General Rommel, whom he admired greatly," said Ken. "He equipped all of us with Volkswagens so we became a complete mobile unit driving around Ireland finding locations. I spent weeks being chased through fields by bloody bulls. I was going crazy but this was Stanley's character - with all his fears and anxieties he was relentless."

When Letizia, Ken's wife, flew out to Ireland she was shocked at his state of mind and persuaded him to return to England and see a doctor for the sake of his health.

"So I was in hospital in England with a breakdown," he continued, "Stanley rang the hospital every day to see how I was doing and if I was still alive. The day I left he phoned me at home. He said: 'Ken, you were right: we're going to change the way we're making the film and you'll love it. I'm sending a second unit to Potsdam in Germany to pick up extra material and I want you to direct it.' Well I found that idea such a huge shock I had to go straight back to the clinic and check in again!"

Despite their friendship and working relationship, Stanley did in fact suggest to me that Ken be removed from the payroll when he was in hospital, to save the production money, and allow his art director Roy Walker to take over. He could be rather cold at times.

It's no wonder after *Barry Lyndon* Ken said his admiration for Kubrick was such that he would never work with him again.

At the end of the shoot I heard Warner boss Frank Wells was flying over from Burbank with other executives, as Stanley wanted to show him something but it was on the proviso that they spent two days in London in their hotel room first. You tell me why!

Frank arrived at Pinewood after spending a couple of days holed up in London, and we went over to the viewing theatre where Jan Harlan met us, and showed us ten minutes of the movie on Stanley's instruction.

Afterwards in my office Frank said, "That was marvellous."

"Yes Frank," I chipped in, "but I don't think I've ever seen a film that didn't have at least ten good minutes of footage in it somewhere."

"That's a point Paul," he said as his facial expression changed from one of delight to one of slight puzzlement.

But that was Stanley!

Warner's never saw rushes on any of Stanley's films, nor the first assembly cut. They only ever saw the final cut that Stanley delivered, by which time it was too late to do anything as release dates and publicity were all locked in. It was a fait accompli. On any other film, the executives would certainly be blunt in offering their thoughts and criticisms, perhaps even ordering re-shoots. But aside from perhaps a gentle suggestion that "It runs a little too long Stanley" from one of the executives, they didn't dare risk upsetting their Maestro nor indeed suggest that they might know better than him.

There aren't a huge number of directors who have the final cut at major studios. Brian De Palma was one such director I worked with, on *Mission: Impossible*. He had it written into his contract and I know as soon as shooting wrapped he 'disappeared'; we later discovered he'd taken a bungalow at the Skywalker Ranch near San Francisco to essentially lock himself away (from external interference) to edit the film his way. We had no idea how long he'd be and I remember Tom Cruise saying, "If he doesn't get on with it I'll take it away from him."

I said, "But you can't, he has final cut."

"What? Does he?" asked Tom somewhat surprised, realising he'd just have to sit and wait for the director to deliver his cut.

I guess Spielberg, Scorsese and Eastwood are among a few directors who can exert such sweeping control nowadays, and that's exactly what Stanley Kubrick had with Warner Bros. Though unlike Eastwood, who always said to me "I feel like I've borrowed money from a bank and I need to repay it" when the studio funded his pictures, Stanley had taken the money from his bank and didn't particularly consider repaying it to be his first priority. Of course he wanted to make a successful film, and he would have got a flat fee for directing so the extended shooting schedule didn't benefit him in terms of overages (that would have broken Warner's!), but ultimately Stanley made films the way Stanley wanted to.

In the event I felt the film was so long and uncommercial; in fact initial reviews were very mixed and it was by no means a box office success. Stanley was awarded the BAFTA that year and it picked up other awards in design, costume and cinematography. It's since been hailed as Stanley's best film and a masterpiece by many critics.

# 1974

## *Bethune*

Every now and again a project came in to Warner's that sounded very interesting, and was certainly worthy of further investigation.

One such story outline was based on the life of Norman Bethune, a Canadian doctor born in 1890, who was credited with introducing modern medicine to China and in developing mobile blood transfusion services in the Spanish Civil War. He in fact became a hero in China and after his premature death in 1939, Chairman Mao published an essay *In Memory of Norman Bethune*, documenting the doctor's final few months, which became required reading and which established the late doctor as a national hero. In fact 'The Norman Bethune Medal' is still the highest medical honour in China.

Ted Kotcheff, a Canadian-born director who was very familiar with the story, was keen to make a film about Bethune. I flew to China for three weeks with Ted to check out the viability of a shoot there, and I remember when news broke of the Terracotta Army having been discovered we realised it was at one of our proposed locations in Xi'an. It was a huge event, and the local farmers who had discovered the 8,000 soldiers, hundreds of chariots and horses, were famous overnight. I felt so privileged to be there as it unfolded but thought, as I saw the huge tarpaulins coming in to cover the area, "It'll be a nightmare to film here now."

The Bethune story was certainly very interesting but Warner's decided it wasn't a particularly commercial film, and moreover, trying to make a film in Red China was going to be inordinately difficult; while we were there on recces alone we had the army accompany us twenty-four hours a day and were not allowed to stray beyond a pre-agreed journey.

The film was shelved.

# 1975

## *Operation Daybreak*

This was the true story of World War II Operation Anthropoid, the attempted assassination of SS General Reinhard Heydrich, the Reich protector of Bohemia and Moravia in May 1942.

The studio had long before decided if the movie was made, then the budget should be kept relatively low, as it was deemed to likely be only a moderately successful box office hit given the specific subject matter, but nevertheless an important film for them to make - underlining that prestige sometimes outweighs commercial returns! For total authenticity, everyone agreed it should be filmed at the actual locations in Czechoslovakia. Happily director Lewis Gilbert was signed and we were set to be the first major international film to shoot in Prague.

During the pre-production period we visited Lidice, just northwest of the capital, which was the village the Nazis wiped out as retribution for the assassination - although Heydrich had survived the initial attack on his car, he died from his injuries in hospital later on - and without question it was one of the saddest places I've ever been to. With the village suspected of harbouring resistance fighters, the Nazis ordered all 173 men, over the age of fifteen, to be murdered and another eleven who were not there at the time were later arrested and shot too. Several hundred women and over a hundred children were sent to concentration camps and four pregnant women were forced to undergo abortions.

The village was torn down and not even the bodies in the cemetery were spared; the remains were ordered to be dug up and burned. Pets and cattle were slaughtered.

It was a massacre.

Only a small percentage of women and children returned from the camps after the war ended and as you might expect, it felt terribly eerie as we stood in the village, imagining the horror that the poor villagers endured.

Being the first major international film in the country was not without its problems. The scale of our physical requirements was far greater than the local film industry had ever encountered, and their being under Communist rule meant that availability of everything - from cans of paint to scaffolding - was a complicated matter. Restaurants and hotels left a lot to be desired and the studio canteen usually served us chicken soup - without much chicken but with added grease floating on top.

But nothing stopped Lewis shooting and keeping everything on schedule; that is until one Saturday afternoon when we were filming outside the church in Lidice and Lewis suddenly stopped. The light was beginning to fade and I was worried there was an issue in getting the very last shot. I asked Lewis what the problem was.

"I'm just getting the football results over the radio, dear," he replied.

It's a good job he supported Arsenal, as the results came through in alphabetical order meaning we lost very little time waiting and got the shot in the can before we lost the all-important light.

It was, as always with Lewis, a very rewarding and happy production.

ALEXANDER SALKIND PRESENTS MARLON BRANDO • GENE HACKMAN IN A RICHARD DONNER FILM

SUPERMAN

STARRING CHRISTOPHER REEVE • ALSO STARRING NED BEATTY • JACKIE COOPER • GLENN FORD • TREVOR HOWARD • MARGOT KIDDER
VALERIE PERRINE • MARIA SCHELL • TERENCE STAMP • PHYLLIS THAXTER • SUSANNAH YORK

STORY BY MARIO PUZO • SCREENPLAY BY MARIO PUZO, DAVID NEWMAN, LESLIE NEWMAN AND ROBERT BENTON
CREATIVE CONSULTANT TOM MANKIEWICZ • DIRECTOR OF PHOTOGRAPHY GEOFFREY UNSWORTH B.S.C.
PRODUCTION DESIGNER JOHN BARRY • MUSIC BY JOHN WILLIAMS • DIRECTED BY RICHARD DONNER
EXECUTIVE PRODUCER ILYA SALKIND • PRODUCED BY PIERRE SPENGLER • PANAVISION® TECHNICOLOR®
AN ALEXANDER AND ILYA SALKIND PRODUCTION

RELEASED BY WARNER BROS. A WARNER COMMUNICATIONS COMPANY



RECORDED IN DOLBY STEREO™

ORIGINAL SOUNDTRACK AVAILABLE ON WARNER BROS. RECORDS AND TAPES

WARNER SUPERMAN BOOKS AT BOOKSTORES AND NEWSSTANDS

PG PARENTAL GUIDANCE SUGGESTED

# 1976-1977

## *Superman - The Movie*

The first Superman film went into production in 1976 but getting the film off the ground proved far more complicated than anyone initially imagined. There were numerous copyright problems that had to be overcome, with script approval as part of the deal with the owners, National Periodical Publications. Then there was the sheer size of the production to think about and, not least, the casting of Superman himself. Fortunately, the producers Alexander and Ilya Salkind were riding the crest of a commercial wave with their box office smash *The Three Musketeers,* and announced Guy Hamilton as their director.

However they'd completely underestimated the cost of the film and faced huge financial problems from day one, from which Warner's bailed them out.

The film was initially set up in Rome, which proved problematic on a number of counts, and not least because after starring in *Last Tango In Paris* Marlon Brando was persona non grata in Italy; but because Brando was deemed an essential part of the production - with a massive $1 million fee - Salkind arranged to hire studio space in the South of France, and said they'd transport all the sets by road from Rome.

The sheer logistics of that would have been a nightmare, and because

**Marlon Brando made cinematic history with his huge pay check for just a few minutes on screen (here with Susannah York)**

all the effects work was to be completed in the UK, it really did make more sense to shoot in London, and would save money in the long run. That's when I boarded the project.

Shepperton Studios was the only facility available, at that point, with the amount of space we needed, and a deal was done. Meanwhile, the film's director, Guy Hamilton, announced that he couldn't work in Britain - for tax reasons - and left the project. He did, however, leave with his full salary.

H stage became the wonderful Ice Palace set, and other construction was underway, but in the few years prior Shepperton had a rocky time with ownership changes and asset stripping, and the place had really not been looked after tremendously well - in fact it looked rather shabby.

This horrified Alexander Salkind, who was very much a showman, and liked to invite distributors and financiers to the studio to show off his production. He said he couldn't possibly bring such important people to such a badly maintained studio and asked we find another studio to relocate the whole shoot! They had already fallen two weeks behind schedule, so this was not good news.

A number of meetings then took place with Cyril Howard at Pinewood, and timings proved just right in so much as the latest Bond film was wrapping, and space was becoming available. We moved the rest of the shoot - and the subsequent two sequels - to Pinewood.

Big names were considered for the title role, including Robert Redford, Clint Eastwood, Steve McQueen, Nick Nolte and Kris Kristofferson; but it went to a relatively unknown actor, Christopher Reeve.

New director Richard Donner initially felt Reeve was too young at twenty-four, but once he had beefed himself up and visited make-up and costume, he was declared the perfect Superman. He could play the dashing

**Enjoying a game of golf with my old friend, and longtime Pinewood MD, Cyril Howard**

**Christopher Reeve as Superman**

hero one moment and then switch deftly to his unsure, bumbling alter ego Clark Kent the next. "I didn't find him," said Donner. "God gave him to me! He looks more like Superman than Superman, and more like Clark Kent than Clark Kent."

*Superman - The Movie* was intended to be the first in a long-running series. In typical Salkind fashion, part of the first sequel was to be filmed at the same time, which meant existing sets could be utilised and actors' salaries minimised. Salkind had recently done this with the sequel to *The Three Musketeers,* much to the displeasure of the actors, who realised too late that they had unwittingly made two films for the price of one.

The pressure was on to catch up with the schedule and there was soon talk of a rift developing between Donner and the producers. At one point later on they tried to sue him for taking the film over budget, which was all nonsense as it was nothing to do with him and I signed an affidavit to that extent for the court. The atmosphere on set was sadly not a pleasant one.

E Stage became the offices of the Daily Planet, the newspaper which Clark Kent and Lois Lane (Margot Kidder) worked for. It was constructed with such attention to detail that American office equipment was brought in by the ton for realism. Officially the schedule allocated two weeks for these scenes, but they became more complicated than envisaged and stretched to five weeks.

Further delays became unavoidable when the casting of the newspaper editor, Perry White, was plunged into turmoil. Jack Klugman pulled out two days before he was due to start and a panic set in to find a replacement. Keenan Wynn was then signed up, but just before shooting the sixty-one-year-old collapsed from exhaustion and was rushed to a London hospital. He was declared unfit to resume work and TV star Jackie Cooper took over, literally being thrust straight in front of the cameras.

The huge lights on the stage placed tremendous demands on the studio generators, leading to a power cut on the main line to Iver. The production was granted an extra day free of charge by Pinewood, but the intense heat of the lights then saw temperatures rise to 100 degrees, causing the emergency sprinkler systems to be activated. Not only were the cast and crew doused, but some of the sets and set dressings were damaged.

With the picture falling alarmingly behind schedule, the Salkinds blamed Donner's over-attention to detail and a serious argument ensued. Rumours swept round the studio that Donner was to be replaced and sure enough the director of *The Three Musketeers,* Richard Lester, was brought in as a producer, numbering Donner's days. The film made Dick's career, though admittedly he'd also just made *The Omen* (a major box office hit) - which Warner's were originally going to back but pulled out of, having produced *The Exorcist II* and feeling they were too similar in theme - and he never looked back!

During all this, *Superman II* was already underway and the pressure was on for super-salary stars like Brando and Hackman to complete their scenes early in the schedule.

One big sequence in the movie was the 'bursting of the Boulder Dam', which was shot on the paddock tank at Pinewood. The set was recreated from photographs of the real dam, complete with its six huge pumps, which pushed water up to the top of the set and over a platform made of reinforced aluminium so that when the dam burst, the water poured over the edge with huge force.

The 007 Stage housed the Fortress of Solitude. Production designer John Barry filled the stage with glaciers and jagged ice peaks. Dendritic dairy salt was used to create the sparkling snowcapped effect at a cost of $6,000.

The crew's belief in the film was justified by its eventual box office returns. *Superman - The Movie* was a massive success, and the rest of *Superman II* was accordingly lined up for shooting. Although, technically speaking, Donner had directed some of the sequel already, he left the series and was replaced by Richard Lester.

I liked Richard Lester and got on with him very well, also he liked to work very fast, which pleased the Salkinds no end; he always delivered his movies a week under schedule. However cinematographer Geoffrey Unsworth said to me, "Dick would deliver a better picture if he was allowed to go one week over schedule."

**The remnants of the Statue of Liberty remained outside a Pinewood workshop for many years**

Another sequel, *Superman III,* was made at Pinewood, though the latter pretty much bombed at the box office and signalled what we all thought would be the end of the franchise. Two years later the Salkinds sold out their interests to Cannon Films.

Warner Bros. were concerned the franchise would suffer at the hands of Cannon and its budget conscious owners Menahem Golan and Yoram Globas, but they were pretty much powerless to act as they were tied in to a "produced in association with" deal, and they had US distribution rights only.

*Superman IV* was described by Christopher Reeve as "terrible". He only agreed to take part after being offered a deal he couldn't refuse - in exchange for starring in the fourth Superman film, they would produce any project of his choosing, and also promised him story input.

Budgets were cut to the bone and as Cannon had thirty other films in production at the same time, they paid no special attention to *Superman IV* at all.

It bombed.

The franchise then lay dormant for two decades.

WILLIAM BLIGH and FLETCHER CHRISTIAN

They were friends through hell.
They became enemies in Paradise.

MEL GIBSON · ANTHONY HOPKINS

# THE BOUNTY

*After 200 years, the truth behind the legend.*

DINO DE LAURENTIIS PRESENTS
MEL GIBSON ANTHONY HOPKINS
"THE BOUNTY" ALSO STARRING EDWARD FOX LAURENCE OLIVIER AS ADMIRAL HOOD
MUSIC COMPOSED AND PERFORMED BY VANGELIS SCREENPLAY BY ROBERT BOLT
BASED UPON THE BOOK "CAPTAIN BLIGH AND MR. CHRISTIAN" BY RICHARD HOUGH
PRODUCED BY BERNARD WILLIAMS DIRECTED BY ROGER DONALDSON

PG PARENTAL GUIDANCE SUGGESTED
SOME MATERIAL MAY NOT BE SUITABLE FOR CHILDREN

DOLBY STEREO® Prints by DeLuxe® Read the Penguin Paperback

An ORION PICTURES Release

# 1977

## *David Lean and The Bounty*

Along with overseeing a lot of films that did get made, I of course was also involved in the early stages of movies that - for reasons of finance, script or creative issues - either never got made, or were put into 'turnaround' - the Hollywood terminology for saying "We'll happily sell the project on to anyone who can reimburse us for what we've spent so far."

One such adventure - and it *was* an adventure - was with David Lean, undoubtedly the doyen of film directors. Many of his earlier films, such as *Great Expectations* and *Oliver Twist,* were shot at Pinewood during my tentative years in the accounts department there, and to this day I feel they are some of the most exquisitely made films ever. The scripts were so textured and with his background as an editor, Lean would really cut a film as he shot it.

Working for companies like Paramount and Warner Bros. meant I was very often invited to functions and whilst I'd met David Lean socially at a couple over the years, it wasn't until 1977 that I met him properly when I was asked to join a meeting in Burbank with the heads of the studio - John Calley, Frank Wells - and David.

They had agreed they were going to make a film of the 'Mutiny on the Bounty' story, though they were quick to emphasize it was not a remake of the Charles Laughton version; this was to be "David Lean's film about The Bounty".

David had been introduced to Warner's through his former agent Philip Kellogg who, having retired from the William Morris Agency, remained close to David and in effect became his producer. I knew John Calley was a huge Lean fan, and so it seemed like a happy marriage.

I was asked to "set it all up" in London, but before leaving California I was invited across to Frank Wells' house, with David, one Sunday to plan out what we were all going to do. David was to go back and work with Robert Bolt in getting the script together, though he told me he felt they really needed a full-sized modern day Bounty - identical in detail to the original, but with an engine in order that we could transport it easier, and a few extra refinements that wouldn't necessarily be evident on screen, but would be useful for us when bobbing about on the ocean somewhere. He also insisted it should have a copper bottom because the coral seas we were going to be in might have damaged a wooden one.

I knew the first thing we needed to do was to get an idea of how much it would cost, and how long it would take, to build the ship as it was a pretty unique requirement.

Frank Wells was, without doubt, the best head of any studio I'd ever worked for and his favourite expression was "got it". Here, he immediately said, "got it Paul", and sent me back to London to meet John Box, the production designer, and together we ended up in Southampton at the big boatyards. There they came up with all the drawings, which of course took time, and in that time the film wasn't really moving forward, which caused David to start getting twitchy as he wanted to start casting and looking at locations.

"If the boat is not going to be ready for eighteen months, then we can't start," I said.

I then went, with our art director Bob Laing who I knew from my early days at Pinewood, on what was really a round the world tour of searching for a place where the Bounty could be built. There was nowhere in England, Scotland or Ireland where they could give us a start date (let alone a date for completion) and so we went further afield to Norway, Sweden, Denmark, Germany, Singapore, Australia and, after some phone calls, we ended up in

**The Bounty takes sail**

New Zealand at a naval shipyard which had just had a major order cancelled and they were looking for new contracts.

John Box, Bob and I flew in to meet and left all the plans with them for a couple of days. Sure enough they called back to say it would take eight months from the day they started, and that was guaranteed.

We called David in Bora Bora, in the South Pacific Ocean, where he was writing away with Robert Bolt, and he flew down to meet us at the shipyard. Whilst I'm not really ever star- struck, I did find the presence and aura which surrounded David Lean to be very exciting. He had such an articulate approach to everything and after discussing every aspect of the ship, he went back to Bora Bora feeling very happy.

John Box and I travelled north to the coast of New Zealand looking for potential locations, and then flew on to join David Lean.

David always had a man named Eddie Fowlie with him. His trade was actually a prop man, special effects technician and even a stunt double, but more importantly he became David's right hand man throughout most of his 'epics' and was credited with creating everything from the Siberian ice palace in *Dr. Zhivago* to quicksand in *Lawrence Of Arabia.* That first evening we were all together in Bora Bora, Eddie joined us at dinner.

"While you have been in New Zealand," David said to John and me, "we have found what I believe to be the perfect location for the Pitcairn Islands. I think we'll get a little plane out there, whilst you're here, and we'll show you."

We'd only just arrived, but such was David's energy that he couldn't pause.

He then added, "Would you meet with Eddie in the morning as he has the budget all worked out."

"What do you mean?" I asked, "What budget? The prop budget?"

"No, the overall budget. I know we have to bring it in under a price, so we will," he replied.

"But David, how can Eddie do a budget? We don't have a script, we don't have a schedule and we haven't finalised the cost of building the Bounty. I don't think there is any point in my looking through Eddie's paperwork."

David obviously didn't want to discuss the matter anymore, so I felt it was pointless arguing and agreed to look through everything Eddie had put together, the next morning. Quite frankly it may as well have been written by my milkman - it was pointless and totally unworkable. I suppose it was David's way of trying to assure the studio, but it didn't wash with me. I guess you could say I didn't get off to the best of starts with David Lean; but it was about to get worse!

A day later we caught a tiny five-seater plane, landed on this grass strip in Rangiroa in the evening and David told us to be ready to board his boat at 7am the next morning. This island didn't have any electricity, though there was a generator which a man turned by hand to give us some light in the evening whilst we had a meal. The bedroom, such as it was, where I was later shown to, was built on stilts - though it couldn't be more different and basic to the holiday villas you see in the Maldives! - and there was a hurricane lamp for light.

John Box, Eddie Fowlie and I turned in, and conscious of not wanting to be late, I got up at 6am and jumped into the shower, without thinking it was only cold water in the pipe, and jumped out just as fast shivering with cold. As we were only expecting to be away for one night, none of us took much gear aside from our toiletries, a spare shirt and clean underpants and socks. When I opened the little wardrobe to get my trousers all that was hanging in there was the belt, waistband and pockets. So I'm standing there in my underwear, scratching my head. I popped around to John Box's room, and he said, "I didn't think we were leaving until 7am?"

"I know," I replied, "but something has eaten my trousers."

"Have you been drinking Paul?"

So I held up the waistband, and I'll never forget John's wonderful response:

"There's nothing I can do Paul, I'm the Production Designer not the Costume Designer."

So there I am, at 6.15am on an island in the middle of nowhere without any trousers. Thankfully, one of the locals let me have a pair of shorts and by 7.20am we were off and running on David's boat where we were to have breakfast.

Sandy, who was David's companion and future wife, was steering the boat and we were bashing across the waves whilst trying to eat and talk, but I was very wary about just how long this trip was taking. By 11am we were still going, with no land in sight. One of my telling characteristics is that when I'm not happy, my face shows it. I'm very easy to read in that respect, and I'd certainly be no good at poker.

David Lean can see that Hitchcock is not too happy, and asks, "What's the matter Paul?"

"This seems a long way to the island David, how much further?"

Just like Captain Bligh, he pointed in front and said, "Just in the distance, just in the distance."

It was now, at least, midday and one of the crew leapt into the water and killed what appeared to be a small shark. Sandy looked over and said, "We always lunch on the boat."

Next thing this chap is gutting the fish and starts to cook it, which of course irritates me further as I'm looking at my watch thinking about the practicalities of such a remote location with a huge film crew, and actors, and all they're seemingly bothered about is lunch.

"David, we've been travelling four and a half hours and we haven't even seen the island, how on earth are we going to film here?"

"What do you mean?" he asked.

"Well your boat is hopping across the waves fairly quickly David," I replied, "we're going to an uninhabited island without any accommodation so this is looking like a daily journey location, unless we bring in a liner. This just doesn't make sense, and is going to be a major expense."

David was unaware of Frank Wells telling me that he "did not want this to be a runaway production" because, with the best will in the world, David had developed a reputation for being extravagant and I know on *Zhivago* the MGM executives had almost daily meetings about the spiralling costs, not least when the production shipped out to Finland when there was no snow to be found in Spain or Mexico, or wherever they were. Fairly, or unfairly, David - with *Lawrence* and *Zhivago* - had developed this reputation of perfection, no matter the cost.

I know David felt as though I'd betrayed him by questioning his judgement, but what he didn't realise was Frank Wells was on my back to ensure the film was brought in on a reasonable budget; to be honest, Warner's wanted to make the film because it was a David Lean film, it wasn't because they had blind faith in the subject matter - if anything they felt it to be borderline commercial - and so their purse strings were never going to be infinitely long.

David later wrote that he felt "conned" by my presence in Tahiti, saying he was just showing me the sights and never thought I would be "drawing up a budget" in my mind and furthermore blamed the studio for assigning me to the project when I was "not an outdoor type". I never actually went to Tahiti with David, but let's not split hairs.

Anyhow back on board David stood up and shouted, "Turn the boat round. Hitchcock thinks this is a waste of time."

Now, David could be tremendously charming but by the same token, when crossed, he could be very difficult. I understood this was a project very dear to him, but I also understood Warner's did not have a bottomless bucket and my loyalty had to be to the company who employed me. When we arrived back in Rangiroa it was getting dark, so we had to race to get to the airstrip and get the plane in the air before we lost the light. We were picked up from the boat in an old beaten up Land Rover and David sat in the front seat. When we pulled up alongside the plane I jumped out and opened the door for David.

"What are you doing, Hitchcock?"

"I'm opening the door for you, David."

"I'll tell you if I want to get out," he snapped.

The flight back to Bora Bora was a very unhappy one and we were all silent. I decided I'd leave the next day, as did John Box, and I subsequently discovered that John was very worried about filming there too; it didn't have the facilities or expertise he needed, and materials were all so very expensive. He told David of his apprehensions, and Lean looked directly at him and asked, "Are you going to return?"

Despite John asking for time to talk with his wife back home, David demanded an immediate answer. The only answer John could give under those circumstances was "No". John later admitted he'd found David to be very "grandiose" and said, "If you can't be God, be a film director."

I noted all of my concerns and delivered them in my report to Frank Wells, but those aside, on arriving back in LA John Box spoke to his former agent Bob Shapiro, who was now head of production at Warner's, and of course rumours spread like wildfire that David was a loose cannon.

Matters weren't helped when I discovered John Calley - who always wanted to be friends and have a great relationship with the talent - had given David my confidential report, in which I expressed various misgivings. My candid reports were only ever intended for the studio heads to read, so I found myself in a position with David Lean that was fast becoming unworkable. He saw me as the villain, and John Calley as his close friend.

Well, Calley's favoured relationship soon came to a head when David next told the studio he wanted to make two films of the story - the first being the mutiny called *The Lawbreakers* and the second being the Pitcairn Island court martial called *The Long Arm.* Calley was aghast and said he only wanted to commit to a one-part film. Anyone else would have thought things through and weighed it all up, but not David - he wanted to do a two-parter or be out of the deal.

Calley responded, "Give us our money back, let us off the hook and you can."

Much to his surprise David replied, "Absolutely."

It was then Calley realised just how out of control it was becoming, just as I had feared in my written report.

The project was put into turnaround and David announced another backer in the shape of Dino De Laurentiis, saying he had found a producer who didn't "have a lack of confidence" in him.

David continued working on the project with DeLaurentiis, eventually deciding to make just the one film, but a series of setbacks and disasters - including losing producer Phil Kellogg, and Robert Bolt suffering a stroke - plagued the film and David was forced to leave the project. Eventually Roger Donaldson directed the picture, which starred Mel Gibson and Anthony

Hopkins, and they used the Bounty which I'd commissioned in New Zealand - and paid the $4 million price tag for it.

Years later, when I was making *Mission: Impossible II,* I saw the Bounty moored up in Sydney Harbour, then a tourist attraction. We went out on it for the day; it brought back a lot of memories and I was able to fill the owner in on its history.

David Lean was so upset with me that we never spoke for years, that is until I saw him in the Pinewood restaurant one day and he wanted to tell me about his next planned film.

(See 1985, *Nostromo*)

## *The Squeeze*

When we were setting up this London gangster film, with director Michael Apted, Warner Bros. had heard about a very popular young comedian named Freddie Starr who they thought would be very good in it. Starr was 'discovered' on the UK talent show *Opportunity Knocks* as an impressionist, singer and comic. He became a huge personality with his own TV show in the 1970s.

Anyhow, they asked I meet with Freddie in London, to find out if he was interested in making movies, and would perhaps be interested in signing a multi-picture deal... but they didn't want me to go through his agent; they wanted me to discuss it with him direct.

I arranged to meet Freddie for lunch in London, and after sitting down he said, "Go ahead and order."

So I did, and then asked him what he'd like.

"Oh, I'm not going to eat," he replied.

One of the worst situations I think you can find yourself in is when this happens because you've got a plate of food in front of you and become very conscious about eating anything. He eventually said he'd have a cup of coffee and when the waitress brought the espresso over he asked, "You don't have anything smaller do you?"

His humour was certainly off the wall, but he also struck me as being a bit unstable. I don't mean that in any nasty or negative way, but you couldn't have a serious conversation with him because he felt he had to put on this persona he'd developed. That concerned me. I told Warner's about my reservations and we agreed the decision should be Michael Apted's to make. In the event he cast Freddie and it all ran smoothly, but it didn't really do much in terms of launching a film career for him.

STANLEY KUBRICK COLLECTION

STANLEY KUBRICK'S

# THE SHINING

# 1979

## *The Corn Is Green*

Occasionally I don't have too much to say about a film, and *The Corn Is Green* is one of those happy examples - I say happy because it was an absolute dream and everything ran like clockwork.

It was based on an Emlyn Williams play and Katharine Hepburn played a strong-willed teacher, determined to educate the poor and illiterate youth of an impoverished Welsh coal mining village in the 1940s, and discovering one whom she believes to have the seeds of genius in him.

It was made on a very modest budget, for television, and director George Cukor - famed for *A Star Is Born, The Philadelphia Story* and *My Fair Lady* amongst other films - was signed on. He was professionalism personified.

The only slight problem came when we left the studios in Wembley to head for the village in Wales, where we discovered modern day TV aerials on roofs everywhere. Every single one needed to be removed to preserve the period nature of the village, but I have to say the villagers were very understanding and we replaced them all afterwards.

It received two Emmy nominations, including Outstanding Lead Actress for Katharine Hepburn.

## *The Shining (1979-1980)*

In 1974 I worked on a film called *The Abdication* with a producer named Robert Fryer; he had a company which had bought the rights to Stephen King's book *The Shining* and he sent me a copy to read, asking if I thought it would make a good film. I said yes it would, but the problem with the book, as with *Empire Of The Sun*, is that when you're reading what a child is thinking, it is very difficult to translate that to the screen. That was my only reservation.

Anyhow, Robert told me he'd submitted it to Warner's and within a very short time he rang me to say he had great news and would be coming over to the UK to produce the film with Stanley Kubrick.

"You're going to produce it with Kubrick? Are you sure Bobby?" I asked.

"Oh yes, I'm signing the deal..."

"Bobby, I'd bet you all the money in the world that all you'll get is a fee, and you won't see a foot of that film until it's released at the cinema," I told him, "and you'll never be allowed on the set."

"I'm not going to do it then!"

"Hang on, you're not going to take a big fee for the film?"

He did in fact take the fee and didn't come near the studio at any time during the production!

Stanley chose stories that intrigued and interested him and in the case of this one, he thought the best-selling book would make an equally very successful movie. He was keen to cast Jack Nicholson, a huge star, in the movie; this was quite a departure for Stanley as although he'd always worked with very good actors he didn't often cast A-list stars. This also added to the budget quite considerably, so it was little wonder Warner heads Bob Daly and Terry Semel were quite insistent that before they'd green-light it they wanted to read a script. They flew into London and I accompanied them to see Stanley at his house near Elstree - it was one of those places where you'd pass through the gate and then drive for two days to reach the front door - and the house itself is full of moviolas and lights, and cables everywhere. It was so cold in there. Stanley asked if we'd like coffee, produced a thermos flask and poured out what was really totally undrinkable sludge.

**Stanley Kubrick and Jack Nicholson, deep in thought during filming**

So here were the two heads of a major Hollywood film studio, sitting shivering with cold and drinking black sludge. In fact I had to take my overcoat off as Terry was shaking so much with the cold I thought he'd pass out. He wrapped it around his legs, and tried to turn the subject around to the script.

**Here's Johnny!**

"Terry," Stanley said, "haven't you bought the property next door to your house in Bel Air?"

"Yes, I have the whole house."

"What sort of security do you have there?" Stanley asked.

Terry, who wasn't at all interested in such things, shook his head and said, "Oh, a fence and alarm..."

"Do you have a gun?" Stanley asked.

"No, but I'm thinking of getting one."

"Oh! Do you know what one you might buy?" he asked enthusiastically.

Again Terry wasn't really interested and shrugged.

"Well what do you want to do if someone breaks in? Do you want to blow them away? Or just frighten them?"

Terry couldn't really answer, so Stanley leapt up and asked, "Have you seen the gun you'd like?"

"No," Terry replied.

"Stay here!" Stanley said, and disappeared for a couple of minutes only to re-appear as though he was about to go off to war, with hand guns and shotguns strapped all over his body.

"This one would only be any good if you got up close... but this one is better at a distance..."

Terry feigned interest and this must have gone on for a good few minutes, before Stanley took them out of the room to put them away. When he returned, he said, "Well, I must get on. Thank you for coming," and escorted us to the front door. We never discussed anything to do with the script!

But that was the control Stanley exerted over the studio. They funded him and couldn't have any say nor insight into what he was doing until such time as *he* was ready. In fact, when I talk about funding Stanley, we paid all his bills each week and did so from the day I started at Warner's until the day he died.

I remember on another occasion during this period Stanley invited the executives to dinner and spoke to his production designer, Roy Walker, about making sure they had some top quality plates and cutlery at the house. Roy's set dresser went over, put on a nice table cloth and laid it all up, and Roy asked, "What sort of food will you be serving?"

"Chinese," Stanley replied.

"Chinese?! How can you cook Chinese?" Roy asked, knowing Stanley didn't employ a chef.

"My driver will go down to Borehamwood and get a selection from the takeaway, and then he'll prepare it on the plates and serve it."

And that's what he did...

Personally I'm not sure Stanley ever had a complete script when he started filming. He never really complained about the various stoppages and delays we encountered with insurance claims on each film and I think that's because it bought him time - time to review where he was, what he'd filmed and what he had left to do. He'd then work on the script accordingly.

That isn't to say he wasn't meticulously prepared, he always was - at least in his mind. He had storyboards and knew exactly how he wanted to plot and shoot a scene. He just didn't necessarily commit it to paper.

**Jack Nicholson with Danny Torrance - young Danny wasn't aware he was making a horror film until many years later as Stanley shielded him.**

Stanley set up offices at Elstree Studios, again local to his home, where the majority of the interior shots, and even some of the exterior shots were completed.

One of the recent innovations at the time was the Steadicam, and Stanley was very keen to use it in this film. Essentially it's a stabilizing mount for a camera, which independently levels out the operator's hand-held movement from the cameras and thereby allows smooth tracking shots. Of course Stanley made modifications and one of the famous shots in the picture is the tracking sequence that follows Danny Lloyd as he pedals at high speed through corridor after corridor on his Big Wheel tricycle. The Steadicam was mounted on a wheelchair and the operator sat in it (with the sound recordist) while pulling a platform rig. The tyres blew out almost causing a serious accident, so solid tyres were next added along with a speedometer so as to duplicate the exact speed of any given shot, take after take.

Principal photography took over a year and actress Shelley Duvall didn't get along very well with Stanley, frequently arguing with him on set about lines, her acting techniques and other things. Duvall actually became physically ill for months and her hair began to fall out.

With ever-changing scripts the star, Jack Nicholson, had to really change his way of working (and in fairness, did so very willingly and helpfully) and learnt most of his lines just minutes before filming them.

I wasn't on set enough to know how the actors regarded Stanley, but I certainly got the impression Stanley didn't have a great deal of time for them. They were pawns in his game of chess. There was never any great warmth or small talk between him and any actors, that I was aware of.

It was not a happy set, to be honest, with cast and crew.

Admittedly, even with a year's shooting, Stanley's overheads were much more modest than other director/producers' as were his running costs, as he never employed big crews nor too many expensive actors; but as most actors were (for some reason) just honoured to work with him that didn't bother them. Consequently the cost of ten weeks on a Kubrick film was probably comparable to five weeks on another studio film.

Incidentally, the insurance claim on this film was due to a stage – which contained one of our major sets - burning down, causing everything to be halted whilst it was all settled.

# 1980

## *The Thorn Birds – the film that never was*

Around 1979/1980, Warner's decided they were going to make a film of the best-selling book *The Thorn Birds* with Robert Redford leading the cast and Herb Ross directing.

As it was all set in Australia, I packed a couple of bags and flew down there with designer Al Brenner to look at setting it all up. We started off in New South Wales looking around at locations for about four weeks, and by the end of our scouting had two suitcases packed full of dirty laundry - we were never in one place long enough to wash anything, so we bought a T-shirt here, and another one there.

Arriving back in LA, I thought my first stop would be at the hotel laundry but we were met at the airport by a unit manager from the studio and he presented me with a letter, which basically said, "While it's all fresh in your mind, we think you should scout California to see if we could find an alternative to Australia."

I left my two bags in a luggage locker and started travelling the length of the state - San Jose, Baton Rouge and just about everywhere else - despite knowing we'd never find anything on the scale we needed to double Australia, and when you're on a big film with Robert Redford, cutting corners and taking second best is not an option, but like a good soldier I did what was asked of me.

Then I was asked to fly to Sicily to meet Herb Ross, who was directing *Nijinsky*. Of course I picked up my dirty laundry first.

Flying to Italy, we found ourselves right in the middle of a strike, so had to divert to Naples where I was told I could catch a boat. With all my notes, photographs and storyboards under my arm I finally arrived in Sicily to meet our director.

"I hear there's a problem with the cast?" he said.

"Yes, Australian Equity (the actors' union) is very strong and they will only let us take Redford, saying the rest of the cast have to be local."

To cut a long story short, it became totally impractical for us to shoot in Australia on our terms, and as there was no decent alternative location, the project folded. Mind you a TV producer named David Wolper, who'd had great success with *Roots*, picked it up and made it as a mini-series starring Richard Chamberlain.

# 1981

## *So Fine*

Ryan O'Neal starred in this film about a New York dress manufacturer who accidentally creates see-through blue denim jeans. The sexy new-style garments become the must-have piece of clothing and solve the company's financial woes, so we head towards a happy ending.

I was asked by Warner Bros. to set up a couple of days' shooting in Venice, which of course would not normally be a problem, but they'd scheduled to shoot these few last scenes over Easter. I contacted my usual Italian production manager, Mario Pisani, and asked him to head across to Venice to set things up. Mario then rang me to say the only way we were going to be able to shoot on Good Friday would be by paying off the shop keepers, gondoliers, local police etc. - in cash!

He asked I take over $45,000 on the Thursday prior in readiness. As I saw it, we had no option. I trusted Mario so I knew if he said this was the only way, then this was the only way.

I duly flew in and checked in to the Gritti Palace Hotel, which I've always believed to be the most glamorous and pretty hotel in Venice, and put the cash straight into my room safe before meeting Mario. He told me we'd been invited to a pre-shoot dinner with the director and cast; it really was a marvellous dinner! It was very late when I retired to my hotel, and I agreed to meet Mario at 7 o'clock the next morning with the money, so we could pay-off the various people.

The next morning I couldn't find the safe-key and after checking and re-checking I went down to speak to the front desk to ask if they had a duplicate key. I was informed, "No, there is only one."

Mario arrived in the lobby, looked through my room, my pockets and anywhere else we could think of and it was obvious I must have dropped it somewhere on the way to, or back from, the dinner. So we went to the restaurant, but alas couldn't find it, so I told the hotel they'd have to call a locksmith.

"After Easter," was the reply they received from everyone they tried. I explained our predicament and that there was a whole crew waiting to start filming, and they managed to find a locksmith on the mainland who'd agreed to come over. It was then 9am, they'd started shooting and the locals were getting very agitated. Mario calmed them down as best he could, and promised their money was on the way. Thankfully the locksmith arrived soon afterwards and I ran with the cash, as fast as I could, to Mario. Talk about cutting it fine. (Or should that be cutting it *so* fine, given the film title?!)

## *Firefox*

Frank Wells called me one evening at home and said he was coming into London and would be having dinner, on the Friday evening at the Connaught Hotel, with David Lean. He said he'd be finished by 10.30pm, and asked if I'd meet him in the bar.

"Sure," I replied, and sure enough on Friday evening he wandered into the bar and suggested we go up to his room to talk.

"This is an unusual request," he said, explaining they needed a 'bread and butter' film from Clint Eastwood, and went on to say, "we own a book which Clint has read and quite likes, but I need you to convince him we can do it the way he wants to do for the money we have to spend on it."

He handed me a copy of the Craig Thomas thriller, *Firefox*, and asked I

...the most devastating killing machine ever built...his job...steal it!
CLINT EASTWOOD
FIREFOX
Clint Eastwood in 'Firefox'
Executive Producer Fritz Manes · Screenplay by Alex Lasker & Wendell Wellman
Based on the novel by Craig Thomas · Produced and Directed by Clint Eastwood
Original music composed and conducted by Maurice Jarre · Panavision® Color by Deluxe®
DOLBY STEREO
IN SELECTED THEATRES
Read The Bantam Book
DISTRIBUTED BY WARNER BROS
A WARNER COMMUNICATIONS COMPANY
PG PARENTAL GUIDANCE SUGGESTED
SOME MATERIAL MAY NOT BE SUITABLE FOR CHILDREN

read it over the weekend, and on the Monday fly to the Deauville Film Festival to meet with Clint, who was being interviewed there by Barry Norman.

I duly flew in, and after the on-stage interview Clint came across to me, said hello, and suggested we had dinner that night to talk. A little while later, he phoned my hotel to say, "Let's talk a little before dinner," and we met for a drink.

"What do you think about it?" he asked.

The plot involved a former US Air Force Major being recruited to go behind the Iron Curtain and steal a prototype Russian fight jet - the Firefox - but with it being the height of the Cold War in 1981, I knew it would be impossible to film at the actual locations.

"I suggest we look at Eastern Europe, find somewhere you're happy with and then we'll make it all look like Russia."

"OK Paul," he replied, "you arrange for us to go wherever you think, as I've got the Warner's jet here and we can head off there."

Unfortunately the (then) Communist countries of the Eastern Bloc such as Hungary and Czechoslovakia, which would have suited us perfectly in terms of location, were off limits because of the political regimes, so first on my list of possibilities was Vienna. I called the Warner Bros. distribution office there and asked they make the arrangements for us to be picked up at the airport and taken to a hotel in the city. Furthermore I asked they book a car and an English-speaking driver to take us around Vienna the next day; Clint didn't want anyone else with us, he just wanted to scout around.

"This is very interesting," Clint said, "where have you arranged for us to go next?"

Copenhagen, Helsinki and a few other capital cities followed day by day until we returned to London on the following Saturday, and we'd both agreed Vienna was the ideal. Clint was taking the jet back to London as he was attending a Frank Sinatra concert that night at the Festival Hall; he asked if I'd like to go with him, and have a few drinks with Frank. One of the biggest regrets of my life was in saying "No"; I'd actually developed cold sores all round my lips and felt very self conscious, but thinking about it now, how many opportunities would I have of meeting someone like Frank Sinatra?

**Clint on location with his Director of Photography Bruce Surtees**

Clint told me not to worry, but I made my excuses.

When we met up at Pinewood, Clint told me he went backstage to Frank's dressing room and sat chatting with him before he went on. I kicked myself!

Working with Clint was such a pleasure because one of the first things he said to me was, "Paul, when I start a movie I like to think I've borrowed the money from the bank and I want to repay it. I don't want any waste of money."

In fact, I took him to lunch in the Pinewood restaurant and afterwards Clint said, "I don't really want to keep coming in here as people come across to talk, and a 30-minute lunch becomes a two hour one. Where else do you go around here?"

"I go to the Fox and Pheasant pub down the road."

"OK, we'll go there."

Sure enough the next day we drove over to the pub, which along with the bar had a lovely Spanish restaurant attached. "You go in there?" Clint asked.

"No, I sit in the bar and have a Ploughman's lunch," I told him.

"That's fine by me."

We did it so many times, and Clint thought it was absolutely magic. One day though he asked me why nobody there ever said anything to him.

"That's easy," I replied, "all the blokes in here go home at night and say to their wives, 'do you know, I was in the pub at lunchtime and there was a bloke in there who looked just like Clint Eastwood'. No one expects you to be in a Stoke Poges pub."

He chuckled.

Everything was prepared thoroughly and the shoot ran like clockwork, though I do remember one location outside Vienna, where Clint's character was stealing the jet from a hangar and it was a bit of a trek, so I told Clint that I'd arranged for us to go by train.

"Train!?"

"Yes, the drive is terrible, down winding roads and will take forever, but it's only an hour by train," I explained.

Clint happily agreed, and arranged for us to stay at a little hotel nearby for a few nights. The owner was absolutely terrific, and went out of her way to make sure there were hot meals for us on our return in the early hours. On the day we were leaving, she came across to me and started telling me her husband was the Vienna champion pistol shot; she said, "I wonder if Mr. Eastwood would challenge him in our pistol range in the basement?"

I knew this would be the last thing in the world he'd want to do, but I said I'd ask. When I did, Clint groaned and said he really didn't want to, but I pleaded her case a little by saying how wonderful she'd been during our stay and how reasonable her charges were, and this quick favour really would mean the world to her husband.

"Oh, OK then. Organise it and let's get in and out as quick as we can," he replied.

Down in the cellar the targets had been pinned up at the far end, and a pistol lay on the bench. The idea was to pick it up, fire and then place it down again before repeating the sequence a couple of times.

The owner's husband was very much a Captain Mainwaring type of slightly pompous, self-important character; he took his shots and stood back smiling quite smugly, obviously thinking this Hollywood actor didn't stand a chance. Clint took his shots and as the targets were wound back on a pulley system the husband's face was an absolute picture. He looked at both and realised Clint had shot his target dead centre each time. We smiled, thanked them and swiftly left!

That reminds me; I was having a chat with Clint in his office one day during the period we were working on *Firefox* and he said he was gearing up to produce and star in a film called *City Heat* (which was set to move into production in 1982) with Burt Reynolds and that he was thinking of hiring Blake Edwards to direct.

"What do you think?" he asked.

"The only thing I can tell you, Clint, is that the nearest I ever came to being admitted into an asylum was when I worked with Blake Edwards on *Darling Lilli.* At the end of the film, Paramount had to give me two weeks in Juan les Pins, in the South of France, in a villa, because they thought I was losing my mind. I'm not sure he's the guy you'd want. He's not Don Segal. He's not the sort of director I think you're used to."

Roll on a few months and one day my phone rang.

"Hi Paul, it's Clint. You were right about Blake Edwards. The first thing he did was strip the office and bring in his own furniture and paintings..."

Knowing Clint as I do, he is not materialistic in any way; when it comes to making a film he walks into a studio office and as long as it has four walls, a desk and chair he's happy. So it obviously worried him that his director was starting off on this footing.

"Who would you recommend, Paul?"

Without hesitating, I said, "The ideal person is Lewis Gilbert. I've made three films with him."

Clint arranged to meet with Lewis and told me he was "exactly the man" for the job. However, Burt Reynolds - who was riding pretty high at the box office at that point in time - was nervous about a non-American director on such an American story, based around a private investigator and Police Lieutenant reluctantly teaming up to investigate a murder.

In the end Richard Benjamin was hired.

I remained very friendly with Clint and whenever I was on the Warner Bros. lot in Burbank I'd often stop by his office, wondering when we might work together again. That chance came about eight years later on a film called *White Hunter Black Heart* (see 1990).

In 1886, following a shipwreck off the west coast of Africa, an infant child became part of a family of apes who raised and protected him.

As he grew, he learned the laws of the Jungle and eventually claimed the title, Lord of the Apes.

Yet, years later, when he was returned to civilization, he would remain uncertain as to which laws he should obey… those of man… or those of the jungle.

Now the director of "Chariots of Fire", captures this epic adventure of a man caught between two different worlds.

# GREYSTOKE

THE LEGEND OF

# TARZAN

LORD OF THE APES

A HUGH HUDSON FILM Starring RALPH RICHARDSON IAN HOLM · JAMES FOX and introducing CHRISTOPHER LAMBERT
ANDIE MacDOWELL Music by JOHN SCOTT Produced by HUGH HUDSON and STANLEY S. CANTER
Screenplay by P. H. VAZAK and MICHAEL AUSTIN Based on the story "TARZAN OF THE APES" by EDGAR RICE BURROUGHS
PG Directed by HUGH HUDSON

# 1983

## *Greystoke - The Legend of Tarzan Lord of the Apes*

In the very early 1980s Greystoke was a project Warner's wanted to make. It was to be written and directed by Robert Towne, who is one of Hollywood's most successful screenwriters. Production designer John Box and I went out on a recce to Kenya, and started looking for locations based out of the Mount Kenya Safari Club (which was founded by William Holden).

When Bob Towne arrived a few days later we showed him around and suggested some of the places we'd found and all was going well. Then the next day the manager of the club said to us, "Mr. Keshowgi would like you to have lunch with him tomorrow."

"We're really not in for lunch, as we get up and go out early," I explained, and you can say what you like about film people but we really do work long hours. Mr. Keshowgi, it turned out, was going to buy all the land around where we were based and so would be quite important to us if we filmed there; so I had a word with Bob Towne and suggested it might be diplomatic to accept his invitation.

Anyhow, we came back to the hotel for lunch and discovered some neatly laid-out tables in the gardens, but there was no sign of Mr. Keshowgi. Just then we heard a helicopter approaching and, sure enough, it landed in the gardens and out of it came a band - and a belly dancer - who set themselves up and started playing the most dreadful music. Bob was, understandably, very annoyed and wanted to get back on the road. The helicopter then took off again, only to return thirty minutes later with Keshowgi - who was all of three foot tall - and with his wife in tow.

He shook hands with us and I introduced him to Bob and John, and he said, "Well I hope you enjoy the meal," and with that, got back into the helicopter and left. It was one of the most bizarre things ever.

Anyway, Bob returned to LA to finish writing the script then delivered it to the studio, but it was huge - about 300 pages. The typical movie script is around 100-125, so I knew that wasn't going to work and, sure enough, it was all shelved.

Roll forward a year or two when I was in Burbank to set up *Firefox* with Clint Eastwood, and a message came through to Clint's office that the new studio head Bob Daly would like to see me.

Clint - who I absolutely admire, and love working with above and beyond anyone else - leaned across and said, "Let me know what happens." He loved the insider gossip!

Bob Daly, who was very charming, said the usual old stuff about how he was looking forward to working with me, and then announced his first project was going to be *Greystoke.*

"I'm going to make it with Hugh Hudson and David Puttnam, who I think did a wonderful job with *Chariots Of Fire* and I really believe they'd do a brilliant job with this film. We haven't announced it yet, but please get to work with David and Hugh."

They weren't going to use the Bob Towne script, and were bringing in a writer named Michael Austin, though in the event I believe some elements were used, as Bob got a credit, but as he no longer wanted to be associated with the project he changed his name to P. H. Vazak for the purposes of the credit - which was the name of his dog. Ironically, it received an Oscar nomination!

"Oh," said Bob Daly before I left his office, "and we're going to make this film for $15 million."

**Christopher Lambert on the jungle set at Elstree Studios**

"Mr. Daly, we've only just met," I replied, "but there is more chance of tomorrow being Christmas than of us making this movie for $15 million!"

Daly was perfectly pleasant and said, "We'll see how it goes Paul."

Once the script arrived, Stuart Craig came on board as designer and we set up a recce to Kenya. However, Hugh Hudson refused to come with us as he didn't believe it was the right place to make the film - he wanted to go to Cameroon, where nobody had ever been (and I understand why!). The locations were no different and no better than those I knew we could find in Kenya, but it was one of the most corrupt and unsafe countries you could ever have visited at that time, and I knew it was going to be problematic.

We scheduled the script and came up with a budget of $28 million, which was pretty high back then.

I returned to LA on the Friday to discuss everything with the studio; a couple of days later Hudson and Puttnam were to arrive in town and meet us in Bob Daly's office at 9am on the Monday morning. Around 7.30am that day, David Puttnam called my hotel room.

"Paul, I've thought so much about this project and I really don't want to be involved with it. I find the budget is too high, I've never worked on a film of this scale and I'm too worried about it."

I rang Hugh and told him David wasn't going to come and didn't want to do the film, but unfazed he said, "let's discuss it all at the meeting."

I thought I'd better get in early and warn Bob Daly and Terry Semel, but Judith (Terry's secretary) said he was in a very important meeting and couldn't be disturbed. As much as I pleaded she wouldn't let me in - quite often you'll find secretaries are far more powerful and fearsome than their bosses. I never had the chance to say anything before Hugh and others arrived, and of course the first thing Bob said was, "Where's Puttnam?"

"He's resigned from the show," I explained.

"But why didn't you tell me this?"

"I've been trying to get in to see you since 8.15 this morning," I said.

In the end it was decided that Hugh would be the 'producer' of the film but that I would be the producer in charge of the production, working full-

**Christopher Lambert and Andie McDowell**

time with Hugh, though as I was an employee of Warner's I wouldn't get a credit. I was to have the final say in anything related to production or finance, and Hugh would have creative control; a letter was drawn up to that effect.

Setting up the location filming in Cameroon was extremely difficult and costly, but Hugh was adamant it had to be there as no other film-maker had done it before. I remained unconvinced audiences would notice any difference between there and Kenya, but what do I know?

Returning to the UK for studio work, at Elstree, we also had some locations at Blenheim Palace, Hatfield House and Floors Castle in Scotland, which was also the scene of a major run-in I had with Hugh Hudson. We had rain like you've never seen up there, but there was a break in the weather forecast one day, with sunshine predicted. I told Hugh that was the day we'd need to shoot the outdoors sequence with the carriages arriving.

"No, I've planned in my mind to shoot the ballroom scenes."

"We can't," I told him, "we have to shoot outside as it's the only good day we're going to get up here."

He was adamant, and so was I. I told the production office to issue the call sheets for outdoor shooting the evening prior, and returned to my hotel where, of course, Hugh phoned me.

"I'm just getting a car to take me to Edinburgh station and you won't be seeing me again!"

"Fine Hugh," I said, "it's disappointing, but have a safe journey."

"What do you mean?"

"I told you, we are shooting outside tomorrow."

The conversation ended, I arrived on set the next morning and sure enough Hugh turned up, ready to go without a word to me.

Eventually, a rough cut of the film was put together for Bob Daly to see in London, though Hugh Hudson was keen to point out it wasn't finished as he wanted to carry on shooting a sequence where the King of the Jungle met the King of England.

"No way, it's already over two hours," Daly said at a meeting we held at Claridge's Hotel one Sunday.

"You've got to trust me. This is going to be a fantastic sequence," Hudson countered, "you're missing the point of what I'm trying to do here."

With that, Daly leapt from his seat and all but dived across the table at Hugh, grabbed him by his collar and said, "Don't you understand? Trust you? We're already over the budget I wanted to allocate. I agreed to all your casting suggestions whether or not I wanted to, and I let you go to Cameroon. I even gave you Paul Hitchcock full-time to the detriment of other projects I would have assigned him to. So don't tell me I'm missing the point."

Terry Semel, Daly's head of production who was also at the meeting, pushed Bob through the bedroom door in his suite and as he did so, said, "I'll call you tonight Paul, the meeting is over for now."

I left the hotel with Hugh, and will never forget him turning to me saying, with a smile, "I think that went pretty well Paul."

Needless to say, no more filming took place and I don't believe Hugh Hudson worked at Warner Bros. ever again.

In fact I think Warner's were a little nervous of the autonomy they'd given Hugh, as for one of the only times I can remember, we took on a completion guarantor - an insurance against the film running over budget. They'd never have called in the policy, and would have certainly footed the bill for any unforeseen contingencies, but the benefit was that the guarantors put their own man, Denis Holt, on the film and he watched every single penny of expenditure. I knew Denis of old and we worked closely in bringing it in on time and budget.

For all the difficulties involved, including putting years on my life, the finished movie was nearly very good in my opinion - *nearly.*

Stuart Craig, our wonderful production designer, received the news during our shoot that he'd been nominated for an Oscar on *Ghandi,* which we were all thrilled about. One day over lunch I mentioned it to Bob Daly and Terry Semel and they turned to Stu and said, "Sorry we can't vote for you as it's not a Warner's film." Poor Stu was distraught because he then realised members don't necessarily vote for what they think is the best film, it's all political.

A little postscript came towards the end of 1983 when, as is the norm with any large studio, senior staff receive a bonus. Usually, I'd receive a cheque in the post but on this occasion I was at the production office at Elstree, and Terry came in to give me my envelope personally, saying, "This is your bonus cheque", for which I thanked him then Bob appeared, pushed another envelope towards me and said, "And this is your bonus for working with Hugh Hudson."

Chevy Chase, star of European Vacation.
Looking for a car chase in Venice maybe?

# 1985

## *National Lampoon's European Vacation*

This was the second in the American 'Vacation' movie series, starring Chevy Chase and Beverley D'Angelo as head of the Griswald family, who compete in a game show called Pig in a Poke and win an all-expenses-paid trip to Europe.

The film was set up from London to shoot on location in the UK, France and Italy. I was about to leave for Rome, with production designer Bob Cartwright, to meet director Amy Heckerling when I received a phone call from Bob.

"Have you read the new pages in the script?" he asked.

"No," I replied, "why?"

"I suggest you do right away as there is something quite startling in there."

The writers had come up with the idea of a car chase for Chevy Chase - in Venice!

Sadly, it was all downhill from there.

Amy Heckerling met our Italian production manager, Mario Pisani, at Rome airport and asked that after seeing the Coliseum, before going to the hotel, could they "swing by Venice"?

But thanks to a terrific crew we managed to deliver a less than memorable film on budget and schedule.

**Keeping my distance on the set of Ladyhawke**

## *Ladyhawke*

Originally we tried to set up this medieval fantasy film in Prague, but we couldn't find the sort of locations director Richard Donner was happy with. Everything then moved to Cinecitta Studios in Rome where I again engaged my Italian production manager friend Mario Pisani. He in turn employed an excellent crew and when the cast - Matthew Broderick, Michelle Pfeiffer and Rutger Hauer - arrived everything ran like clockwork.

It was beautifully photographed by Vittorio Storaro, making full use of the terrific Italian locations and terrain. When producer Harvey Bernhard had to return to LA unexpectedly, for personal reasons, I took over and spent a considerable time on the stage floor. It really was a terrific film to work on and one without incident. Unlike my next...

## *David Lean's Nostromo*

Warner Bros. had a table in the Pinewood restaurant, in the far corner, and I regularly held lunch meetings there. One day I was standing in the queue of the carvery and noticed David Lean; he'd just been knighted and was finishing up his work on *A Passage To India.*

"How are you Paul?" he asked.

"Oh I'm fine, and many congratulations on your knighthood," I said, feeling perhaps a little awkward. However, I needn't have as he smiled and said, "you know Paul, I've missed our meetings."

That really rather took me aback, and I thought it was a terribly nice way of re-establishing our friendship as I know he was terribly cross with me over the whole *Bounty* project.

"I've been meaning to call you, as I have a project I'd like to talk to you about. May I join you for coffee after lunch?"

The amazing thing was Sir David Lean, arguably our greatest living film director, was sitting not at the very best table but rather at the smallest table in the place, and all alone. I found it tinged with sadness to be honest.

Anyhow, he came across after lunch and explained his agent was about to approach Warner Bros. regarding a film of the book *Nostromo.* I'd read the book years earlier so vaguely knew what it was about, and David continued, "So when you get the phone call we'll get together and start planning it."

A week later, the call came through saying a deal was being made and we should start things moving, but they were still waiting for the script so I was to advance as much as I could meanwhile. Again it was a case of the studio being more interested in working with David Lean than in the particular subject matter - they had a slot in their distribution schedule the next year that it would fit, and that was the main concern.

We set up production offices at Shepperton Studios; David wanted to shoot a series of tests, as he wasn't sure if he wanted to film in 35mm or 70mm and on which stocks. So he decided to compare several options, and when you do a test with David Lean it's not just in an empty sound stage - on

**David Lean**

the contrary it's on the most lavish and expensive set his designer can come up with.

Steven Spielberg had boarded the project as producer for the studio and all seemed to be moving forward.

I'd always considered the book a difficult read, and I really wasn't sure how it would translate to the screen. Later on I discovered David shared my concerns, as he wrote, "I spent most of the 200 pages fighting sleep". Christopher Hampton was engaged as writer, and Spielberg had made quite a few notes on the material he'd read, which annoyed David no end as he didn't anticipate Spielberg having any creative involvement. Hampton, having made little further progress, left the project to work on another film and Lean's long-time collaborator Robert Bolt was hired.

Warner's, wary of the commerciality of the project, started looking for a partner to share half the costs, which again annoyed David as he felt they were only half-heartedly committed, and this led to tension with Spielberg who in turn walked away. Robert Bolt's health was beginning to fail and as the weeks went by, and of course with costs building up, the people back in Burbank kept asking me, "Where is the script Paul? We were promised it was nearly finished."

I really felt they should have phoned David directly and had a conversation with him, rather than sending me in, but that's how studios operate - when there's good news to share, the bosses are straight on the phone to the talent offering their congratulations; but when it's not so good news or they want answers to questions, then they defer to their 'man in London'. Fair enough, I suppose, that's my job but my point is when you're dealing with someone like David, he appreciated the courtesy he felt his position in the business warranted.

I'm not afraid of confrontation nor making a decision, so as gently as I could, I told David we desperately needed the script.

"Oh, I'll speak to Robert, I'm sure it'll be here soon."

Two weeks went by and the call came through to me that Warner's were not funding the project beyond that week, and I was to put everyone on notice unless they had the script. I drove over to see David and I repeated what I'd been told. He felt rather hurt his own studio was not talking to him, but assured me on Friday he'd have eighty-five pages of the script. "I'd like you to take it to Burbank for them to read and hopefully they'll be happy and will continue funding us."

I made arrangements to fly and told Terry Semel, head of the studio, that he'd have the weekend to read it and we'd get together on the Monday morning to discuss.

"Tell us Paul," they said at that meeting, "what happens at the end?"

"David's going to follow the book. Nostromo will die."

"Die!" they gasped, "we don't want the hero to die."

"Well I'm sorry," I replied, "but that's how the book ends."

They went on...

"Some of these characters need to be bigger and brought out... and we're not sure *Nostromo* is the best title."

"But that's the title of Joseph Conrad's book; that's the film David is making," I explained. "It's all in the book."

Clearly, no one had read the book.

"You should fly back this evening Paul, go see David and tell him we think Nostromo should live and we need to think about other titles."

"I'm sorry guys," I said, "but I'm not doing that. I once told him a location was too far and he never spoke to me again for years. You'll find my body in the Thames if I dare go back and say any of that to him. With the greatest respect, you have to tell David as it's a huge, huge thing."

Warner Bros. pulled out of the project.

David continued trying to pull together the finance for *Nostromo* but sadly he died in 1991, and the film with him.

Little Shop of Horrors

# 1985-86

## *Little Shop of Horrors*

Occasionally at Warner Bros. I'd be parachuted into a film that had been developed and prepped elsewhere, and *Little Shop of Horrors* was one such project that had been set up in the USA but, for reasons of cost, was moved to the UK at the eleventh hour.

Frank Oz was directing, and being a veteran of *The Muppet Show* it wasn't only right up his street, with the puppets and animatronics, but on his old patch too - he loved London and had a home there. I have to say he was easily one of the most wonderful directors to work with.

The budget and schedule had all been prepared in the USA, so it became a little bit like an arranged marriage for me in just going along with it, but after a couple of weeks I could see that things were moving much slower than anticipated - in fact we were nearly a week behind. Whoever drew up the schedule hadn't taken into consideration that all the animatronics took a little while to reset, and the maximum shots they were getting were five to six a day but the schedule had anticipated eighteen. You don't need to be a genius to know that even if you work flat out, you're still at least 50% behind.

I called the studio, but they said I was wrong and that Frank should simply work faster.

"He can only go as fast as the puppeteers and animatronics guys," I explained. "If they're not ready, he can't shoot."

But studios never want to hear bad news, they just expect you to get on with it and deliver. Short of tearing pages out of the script, that simply doesn't work. So after three weeks, the studio fired the American producer (well, someone had to take the blame) and sent him home, meaning that I had to then step in and work closely with Frank. The first thing I did was to suggest we work on Saturdays to try and catch up a little.

A few more weeks passed and one Saturday Terry Semel rang me at home, telling me that he found it unacceptable that we weren't working faster. I of course had to relay the conversation, such as it was, to Frank Oz.

"Paul, I'm doing my best," he said. "I'm not a poor man, I have a lovely home and a loving wife so if you'd rather get someone else in to finish the film, that's fine. But I can't do any more."

The next day, Sunday, I was playing cricket at Hampton Court and a message came down from the clubhouse that I was to phone Terry Semel immediately. When I got through, he said, "You didn't call me back yesterday."

"I was going to call you on Monday," I replied, "I spoke to Frank and he's doing his best."

"This is urgent Paul. Would you ask Frank to be in your office at 7pm on Monday and get him on the speaker phone?"

I told Frank, who naturally wasn't terribly pleased because no matter what anyone said, there was no way of working faster. Frank is a wonderfully creative person, but I knew the pressure he was now feeling wasn't something that was going to help anyone.

The call came through, and Terry said, "Hi Frank how are you? Did you have a nice weekend?" and all the usual nonsense, before getting down to the crux of it all, "Paul tells me that he doesn't feel it can be moved on any quicker?"

Frank told him exactly as he told me - that he wasn't a poor man, he had a lovely home and a loving wife and would understand if Terry wanted to bring someone else in. We all knew there was no way anyone else could come in and take the film over, and so it was agreed - albeit reluctantly by Semel - that we'd carry on and finish it as fast as we could.

**Steve Martin and Rick Moranis**

Things became a little clearer to us just after we'd completed principal photography and were moving into post-production - David Geffen, who was the overall producer, arrived in London and came to see me. He asked why it had taken so long to shoot, and said he wasn't very happy with me as he'd had a release date set which had to be pushed back and then he started lecturing me about how quickly other films he'd been involved with had been made.

"Mr. Geffen," I piped up, "there isn't a man alive who could work faster than Frank Oz, but if he gets as many as five or six set-ups a day, then we're lucky."

"Well who is to blame?" he asked.

"Whoever drew up the schedule in the States," I replied.

It wasn't an easy meeting, and left a bit of a bad taste in my mouth if I'm honest. The trouble is studios set release dates for films and, come what may, you have to hit those dates. Unfortunately, it's just not always possible, no matter who promises you the schedule will work.

However the finished movie looked spectacular on the big screen and went on to make everyone a nice return.

A year or so later I was in LA and bumped into Frank at a hotel, and he asked if I was free for breakfast the next morning, which of course I was delighted to be. He told me about his next film, which was called *Dirty Rotten Scoundrels,* and asked if I might be interested in producing. I said I couldn't as I was contracted to Warner Bros. but I knew a good producer, now based in LA, who I'd worked with on some of the Stanley Kubrick films. I introduced him to Bernie Williams and in fact they went on to do a couple of films together.

It became a happy ending to a rather frustrating story.

Incidentally, this was the last film to shoot at Pinewood before it went 'four-walled'. Up until that time Pinewood employed a permanent full-time staff in all the various departments and was a fully serviced studio, but with there being very little booked into the studio Cyril Howard, the Managing Director, found it hard going to meet the huge studio payroll each month and was forced to face the inevitable - the staff of 500 was reduced to 145. Pinewood was the last studio in the UK to go 'four-walled' and even then Cyril had an uphill battle to keep things going, so diversified by bringing TV commercials and pop promos on site; they also encouraged more 'renters' to move in to the many empty offices so production companies, suppliers, agencies, insurers etc. all set up shop at the studio and provided another valuable revenue stream with rent each week.

## *Club Paradise*

Although we set up this film starring Robin Williams and Peter O'Toole in London, we filmed everything on location in Jamaica. It centred around a Chicago firefighter (Williams) being fed up and retiring to a Caribbean island where he frequented a rundown beach resort (run by O'Toole) and together they renovated and reopened it.

However, though I say Robin Williams was cast in the lead we had actually had Bill Murray lined up, but he became unavailable during pre-production and we faced closing the production down; in fact that's exactly what I

PRINCE
Under the
CHERRY MOON

had to fly out there to do. A few weeks later though, I received a call asking me to resurrect everything as Robin Williams had been secured.

It was one of those wonderful locations you often see featured in holiday magazines and programmes, and a very pleasant way to make a film it was too. Sadly, commercial success evaded it.

## *Under The Cherry Moon*

Prince, the pop star, decided he wanted to direct and star in a film about two friends, from Miami, in the Mediterranean, who enjoy life by scamming money off rich women. Everything was duly set up at Victorine Studios in Nice, with locations set for Nice and Cannes and along the Cote d'Azur.

A few days before they started shooting, the producer called me and asked I make arrangements with a UK laboratory to process the rushes overnight, print them in black and white, and ensure they reached Nice by midday the next day.

"I thought we were shooting in colour?" I asked.

"Yes, but Prince wants to see the footage in black and white as he thinks the quality would be that much better," the producer replied.

"Well what about later on, when it comes to release prints?"

"Prince wants the film to go out in black and white," he told me.

"So we are going to shoot in colour, so as to get a better black and white image?"

"Yes," he said, "You've got it!"

Got it I certainly had!

I called Warner's and explained what I'd just been told, and how ludicrous it was to consider shooting in colour, only to watch it in black and white; not only that, the extra time it would take in preparing black and white dailies combined with the extra expense seemed a terrible waste to me. Should the film have been a hit, the cost of arranging thousands of B&W release prints would have been exorbitant too.

I was told to go along with what Prince wanted, and to ensure the B&W dailies were ready each morning for flying to Nice.

After about three weeks Warner's called and told me to scrap the B&W idea, and go ahead as we normally would with colour only. They'd no doubt seen some of the rushes and whether it had been screened in colour or B&W hardly made a difference, as it was voted the worst film of the year!

**IN VIETNAM**
**THE WIND**
**DOESN'T BLOW**
**IT SUCKS**

**Stanley Kubrick's**

# FULL METAL JACKET

WARNER BROS PRESENTS STANLEY KUBRICK'S FULL METAL JACKET

STARRING
MATTHEW MODINE ADAM BALDWIN VINCENT D'ONOFRIO LEE ERMEY DORIAN HAREWOOD ARLISS HOWARD
KEVYN MAJOR HOWARD ED O'ROSS SCREENPLAY BY STANLEY KUBRICK MICHAEL HERR GUSTAV HASFORD
BASED ON THE NOVEL THE SHORT-TIMERS BY GUSTAV HASFORD CO PRODUCER PHILIP HOBBS EXECUTIVE PRODUCER JAN HARLAN PRODUCED AND DIRECTED BY STANLEY KUBRICK

WARNER BROS A WARNER COMMUNICATIONS COMPANY

# 1986-87

## *Full Metal Jacket*

*The Shining*, when finally completed, was critically and commercially well received, yet it was over a decade before Stanley Kubrick started shooting his next movie.

*Full Metal Jacket* was an American war film, set during the time of the Vietnam conflict, and Stanley planned to make it all in England. He duly dispatched scouts everywhere across southern England looking for suitable locations, though once again his reluctance to travel far meant he would only ever really work within commutable distance of his home, so we had to recreate Vietnam at Beckton Gas Works - as only Stanley could!

Keen to cast genuine Americans Stanley launched a national casting search in the USA and had all the auditions videotaped - he received over 3,000 tapes back at the studio. He whittled down likely candidates and then invited them to fly over and meet him.

The gas works, in east London, were due to be demolished and Warner's secured a deal to use the site to recreate the ruined city of Huế, which Stanley had gathered masses of photographs of, from 1968. To achieve the desired look, Stanley had some of the existing buildings blown up, and brought in a wrecking ball to knock specific holes in others. A plastic replica jungle was flown in from California, but once he looked at it Stanley was distinctly unimpressed and instead had 200 Spanish palm trees imported along with 100,000 plastic tropical plants from Hong Kong!

The site itself meanwhile proved a nightmare for the entire film crew as asbestos and hundreds of chemicals had poisoned both the earth and air.

I visited the site a few times, really only to get an idea of when Stanley might start shooting. My weekly reports went into Warner's with my best guess estimates of the budget and schedule, to which we'd add a year for post-production. That would then give the studio an idea of a possible release schedule - though with Stanley, nothing could ever be pinned down specifically. By the end of the shoot, we'd used over 1 million feet of film. I'd worked with directors who'd shot 500,000 feet and thought that was fairly excessive, so you can imagine the task involved in bringing that down to 12,000 to 15,000 feet for the final release print - was a year even long enough?!

There were some really interesting entries into the budget such as four M41 tanks from a Belgian army colonel, Westland Wessex and Choctaw helicopters and a whole arsenal of weapons and rockets. It was as though Stanley was building his own private army.

One night Stanley called me at home and said, "Paul, Lee Ermey has lost his voice. How long does it take for someone to recover and regain their voice - how long would it take for a singer?"

"You mean someone like Streisand?" whom I knew.

"Yes, find out and ring me back."

I left a message with Barbra's assistant, but Stanley kept calling asking if I'd heard back. So in the end I rang a doctor I knew, and asked the question. He suggested it would be something like two to three weeks if it was a condition like tonsillitis.

I called Stanley, and he immediately said, "Then we'll have to close down the film."

So the insurers moved in...

**Vincent D'Onofrio**

Incidentally, I can't ever recall Stanley having a unit publicist on one of his films. It's certainly the norm, and publicists would bring in journalists regularly to the set, release news to the media and compile a range of stills to help promote the movie ahead of release. When I raised the idea of having a stills photographer even, Stanley said, "I will take a print from the negative if I need a still."

He didn't think publicity was a necessary tool for his films.

Many say he was a genius. I'd certainly say he was a very intelligent and extraordinary person, but some of his ideas wasted so much time. One day, for example, he told me he only wanted single people on his crew, because "they don't mind the hours they work."

I said, "Stanley, it's the other way around. The married ones don't want to go home to their wives, and besides they're the ones that usually need the overtime more to pay the bills."

He'd employ people to research minute aspects of things, that really held no importance to the picture, and he'd shoot scenes with an actor and then decide they weren't right, or extend their schedules beyond what they were free to do, and so he'd re-cast and film it all again. I know in his next - and final - film, *Eyes Wide Shut* (which I wasn't involved with but saw being made at Pinewood), he filmed with Harvey Keitel but kept wanting to film more and more; eventually Keitel dropped out as he was contracted to another picture and Stanley re-cast with Sydney Pollack and filmed everything over again. Tom Cruise, whom I'd worked with and was soon to do so again, and his then wife Nicole Kidman signed open-ended contracts for the movie, which only Stanley could release them from when he felt the film was finished. In fact it holds the Guinness Book Of Records top spot as the world's longest ever film production. They shot for 400 days.

Looking back on *Eyes Wide Shut* I now realise what a mistake it was for Stanley. His self-imposed reclusiveness meant that he really didn't have any understanding of the real world apart from what he read or saw on TV and films; so a subject such as this one wasn't something I think he'd feel particularly at ease with. In fact his family would have you believe Stanley was a bit of a prude, as was demonstrated when my (now) wife Lidia, who was a production assistant in 1993, started work for Stanley. The project had the working title *Aryan Papers* and was a Second World War holocaust movie. Stanley had long been fascinated with the idea of making a film about the Nazis and WWII, and had himself adapted Louis Begley's book *Wartime Lies,* the story of a Jewish boy and his aunt in-hiding from the regime.

The film was planned to shoot in the Slovak Republic and as Lidia had knowledge of the language and the terrain, along with production contacts in the country, she got the job. Although Lidia had lived in the UK for nearly ten years, she still kept the old home country customary habits...

At one particular meeting held in Jan Harlan's (Kubrick's brother-in-law) UK home the production team gathered with a potential Czech Production Manager, whose grasp of the English language disappeared the moment he met Stanley in person - he was awestruck. Anyhow, when Stanley arrived Lidia naturally kissed him on the cheek in greeting him. She hadn't realised the rest of the crew just said a polite 'hello'.

**Stanley Kubrick on set, explaining the shot he wants to capture**

She then sat down next to Phil Hobbs (Stanley's son-in law) and was scolded by a whisper from him, "You never ever do that again!"

"Do what?" she asked in all innocence.

"Kiss Stanley. Nobody gets close to him other than his own family."

Lidia was naturally worried she had over stepped the line and had blown her job on the film. When the meeting broke up, Lidia said a quiet and polite goodbye to all present, and Stanley rose from his chair.

"No kiss now?" he asked, with a wry smile.

It certainly broke the icy atmosphere and undoubtedly confirmed Lidia's future on the project. Sadly, after seeing *Schindler's List,* Stanley later cancelled *Aryan Papers* feeling it impossible to better Spielberg's film.

*Eyes Wide Shut,* meanwhile, received very mixed reviews, but in all fairness if I was the head of Warner's and Stanley came to me saying he was going to make a 'sexy film' with two of the biggest stars of the moment, I'd have to take it seriously. It sounded a good idea on paper, but knowing Stanley it was probably his worst idea ever as he was a total recluse and didn't really, outside watching films, understand much about life in the real world. He never went anywhere nor met anyone so how could he possibly make a film like this?

When I was making *MI:2* in Australia with Tom, he had to shoot off every now and again to premieres; when it came to Sydney's turn to host an opening Tom invited me along with John Woo, our director, and afterwards asked what we thought.

I honestly did not know what to say. I thought it was dreadful. I felt sad, because despite all the problems and hassles I encountered with Stanley he was a passionate film maker and it's a huge shame that what proved to be his last film was by no means his best.

## *Frantic* (1987)

When Roman Polanski's planned thriller first came to my attention, I was asked to accompany Rick Senat (WB, Business Affairs Executive) and we met with Polanski and Bruce Berman (WB, Senior Vice President of Production) at a hotel in Paris to discuss progressing the project.

I've always believed - and will keep saying this to the day I drop - the way to make a film successfully and on schedule is by employing the very best people possible, and those you trust. I really didn't like inheriting either people I didn't know, or those I'd heard dubious things about because I've discovered the hard way that it just doesn't work. Key to everything is a good Production Manager and Line Producer - they run the show.

In our discussions, Polanski routinely said, "My Production Manager is so-and-so and I always use him."

"That won't work for us Roman," I said, and I knew him reasonably well having been involved in a few films with him, so felt I could speak my mind. I looked around as I now needed the help of Bruce Berman and Rick Senat to stand my corner, but Berman looked up and said, "We should go with Roman's person. He's done all Roman's films."

With that, he stood up, asked to be excused and disappeared downstairs. A few minutes later he reappeared and said, "Isn't it marvellous. There are no direct flights to LA on a Tuesday."

"I thought you'd know that Bruce. No one flies in Europe on a Tuesday," I explained.

Nearly fifteen years later, Rick Senat sent me a cutting from a newspaper saying "United Airlines now fly Paris to LA direct on Tuesdays"... he'd never forgotten!

Anyhow, going back to Polanski, I sent Terry Semel a memo and explained I had misgivings about the person Polanski wanted to run the film. Terry came back and said, "I think Bruce is right. We need to go with the person Roman wants."

"In that case," I explained, "I cannot be financially responsible for this movie, if I don't have any say on who is appointed."

"With the greatest of respect Paul, it is your job to be responsible."

I wasn't budging on my position, and told Terry so. It could have easily cost me my job I guess, but my argument has always been prevention is better than cure - and I wanted to prevent any unnecessary problems occurring on the picture. A short while later he called back and said he'd spoken with Polanski and I should go ahead and appoint who I felt was best for the job.

One of Terry's plus points was that he did support me in the majority of my decisions. Though Terry did once tell me that he would never back me "in front of the talent", meaning in order to preserve the wonderful relationships with stars, directors and producers he and all other studio executives craved to have; he'd stand up for their point of view ahead of listening to mine. In private it was different of course, but in public I knew when to bite my tongue.

**Sigourney Weaver on location with one of the gorillas**

## *Gorillas In The Mist*

Warner Bros. and Universal Pictures decided to explore the possibility of working together on making a feature film of the story of naturalist Dian Fossey, and her work in Rwanda with mountain gorillas.

I was asked to go to Kigali, the capital city of Rwanda, to see if the Government would grant us permission to film with the apes, and indeed, if permission was forthcoming whether or not it was all practical. Rick Senat, head of Warner Business Affairs, received the same phone call to travel with me, and was told it was important we got there before Universal's representative.

Rick and I were happily first in to meet the Ministers and after many discussions in French (thank goodness Rick is fluent!) an outline agreement, allowing us to photograph the gorillas, was signed.

Before heading back to London, I asked if Rick and I could go up into the mountains to see the gorillas and get an idea of what would be involved from a shooting point of view. That Sunday a representative of the African Wildlife Foundation escorted us on our expedition. After about a forty-minute drive in a very old Land Rover, we arrived at the base of a mountain where we were told the gorillas would be and, following two hours on foot trekking through dense undergrowth, we reached a clearing and saw them - mum, dad and three children. It was the most amazing sight I've ever encountered, and is something I'll never forget.

It was then back to London, and on to LA to report our findings. I felt the only way we'd ever be able to make this movie would be with a very small crew, and to base ourselves as close as possible to the gorillas, so a lot would depend on finding a lead actress who'd be prepared to live under canvas, and indeed be willing to get as close to the gorillas as possible.

We received the go-ahead for what would be a co-production, but one in which Warner Bros. had overall control.

Sigourney Weaver was secured to play Dian and, in my humble opinion, was one of the few leading actresses that could have played the role, and indeed have worked under such tough physical conditions. Bryan Brown was our main male star, playing photographer Bob Campbell.

**Brilliant casting - Sigourney Weaver and Bryan Brown**

Michael Apted, a director I admired greatly, was also signed and in my experience I've rarely known a director who has drawn such terrific performances from his leading ladies. We certainly had the best possible team working on the picture.

Our preparation period was long and hard-going for the crew out in Rwanda, but they all endured the most hazardous of conditions, and then twelve long six-day weeks of shooting; the one luxury being every Saturday afternoon, when the cast and crew loaded up into a minibus and travelled nearly two hours to a small hotel in Gisenyi, where they could bathe, shower, eat in a restaurant and sleep in a proper bed, until they left the following afternoon in readiness for another six day shoot.

From our base camp, at the start of the shoot, it took an average of two hours to find the gorillas in the jungle; but as we advanced through the schedule we found that foot travel time dropped to ninety minutes as everyone was that much fitter!

Local trackers helped us enormously, and the dozens of local labour-

**A publicity shot to melt the heart!**

ers who humped our equipment up and down every day certainly deserve special mention.

Having completed our location filming in the mountains, the unit moved to Kenya and the Aberdares Highland region which had a jungle type terrain, and again the crew were under canvas for the duration. This is where we filmed the shots with Rick Baker's gorilla doubles - and I defy anyone to tell me they weren't real gorillas - as it was too dangerous to attempt it around the real animals. Rick Baker - who I'd worked with on Greystoke - was a remarkably talented technician who created gorilla suits for mime artists to wear, along with some animatronic ones.

On one of my visits to the set I asked Terry Clegg, our producer, where my son Martin (who was Art Director) was.

"Lying down in his tent," was the reply.

It was mid-morning, the busiest time on a set, so I couldn't understand why Martin wouldn't be on set. I found him in his tent, traumatised as he'd been chased by a lion. Michael Apted had asked him to look nearby for a particular location, for the crew to move on to after their current shot, and Martin had set off with three local gamekeepers, armed with old WWI Lee Enfield 303 rifles. Suddenly they heard a roar and saw a pride of lions directly in front of them. The game wardens fired their one shot each and ran off into the jungle, leaving Martin alone with the lioness. Martin literally ran for his life and just made it back to the unit in time for the lion to be scared away by the number of crew standing there. No wonder he was lying down!

With location work in the can, we moved back to Shepperton Studios to complete the interiors.

This was undoubtedly one of the toughest films I've ever worked on, in terms of difficult working conditions and remoteness, but thanks to Michael Apted, Sigourney Weaver and a terrific crew it was the most satisfying experience of my career too.

Shortly after we left Rwanda, a civil war broke out and tragically many of the wonderful locals who had been an integral part of our crew lost their lives.

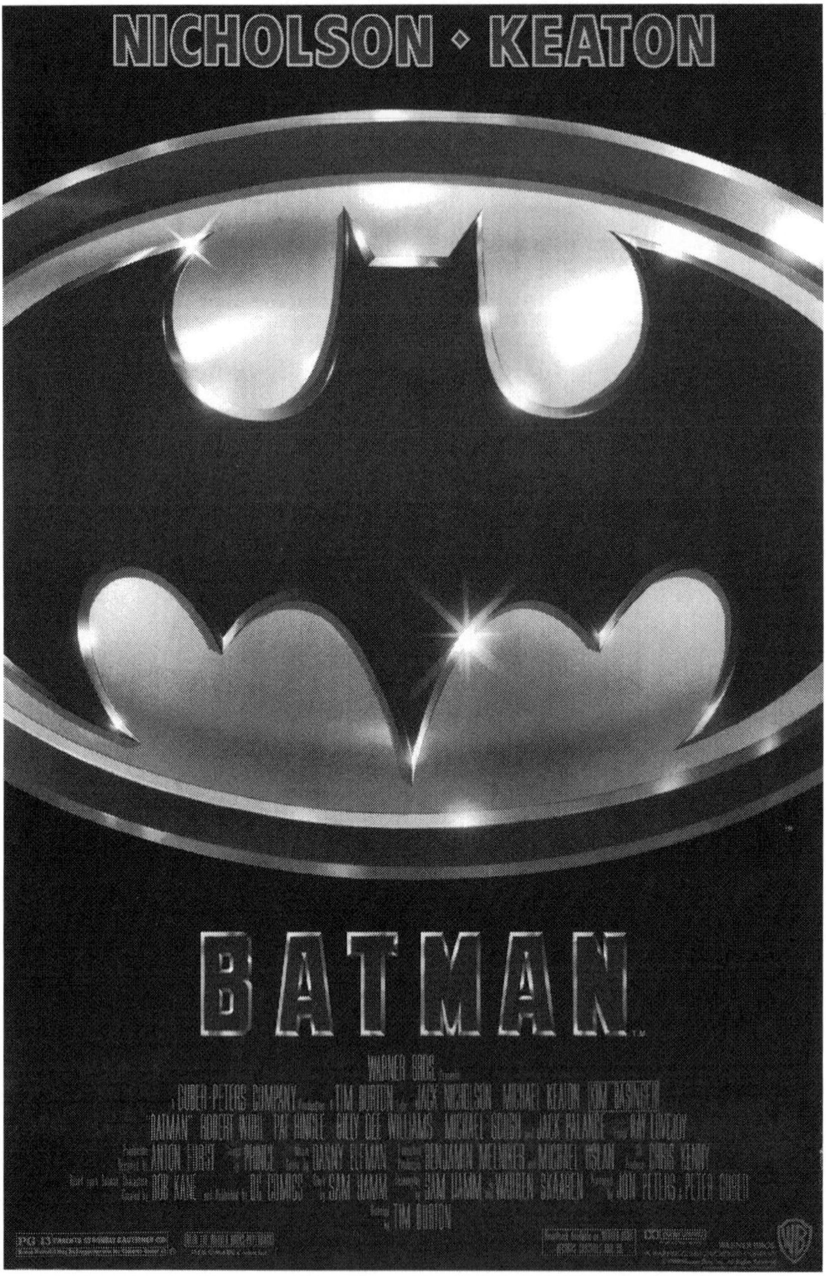
NICHOLSON • KEATON
BATMAN
WARNER BROS.
TIM BURTON

# 1988

## *Batman*

Whilst I was rarely dispatched to far flung locations on the back of a phone call at Warner Bros. any longer, when we were setting up the first *Batman* with Tim Burton I did fly with Tim to Ireland to meet with Derek Meddings, whom Tim was very keen to engage for the special effects work on our film; he was a huge admirer of Derek's work, not least *Superman* for which he won an Oscar. When we flew back though, Heathrow was closed due to heavy fog and we were diverted to Bristol.

"So what's Bristol like Paul?" Tim asked.

I laughed and, thinking about all the exotic places I'd visited over the years, had to admit, "I've no idea. I've never been here before!"

*Batman* had been in the Warner Bros. pipeline for a few years, and Tim Burton had been attached to direct from the off. I know several writers had been involved, and although everyone seemed happy with the script it never quite got the green light; that is until Tim directed *Beetlejuice* in 1988 and made a fortune for Warner Bros. They then thought Tim could do no wrong and gave the thumbs up to *Batman*.

Media interest was huge, and Warner's decided to set the picture up at Pinewood - far from the Hollywood glare - where they could take over most of the studio, as there was precious little else shooting.

Having worked on *Beetlejuice* with Michael Keaton, Tim was keen to cast him as Batman but there seemed to be some doubt as to whether an actor known primarily for light comedy roles could carry off playing The Dark Knight. All sorts of other names were bandied about: Mel Gibson, Charlie Sheen, Kevin Costner, Tom Selleck, Pierce Brosnan and Bill Murray being amongst them. But Tim and producer Jon Peters favoured Keaton, saying he had an "edgy, tormented quality". It is said 50,000 letters from disgruntled fans were sent to Warner's, with them all worrying it was going to be too much like the 1960s TV series with Adam West - kitsch and camp. Little did they know!

The lead villain, The Joker, was the next role to be cast. Brad Dourif was Tim's first choice, and Robin Williams was looming large, but in the end it was offered to Jack Nicholson who, in my opinion, stole the whole film.

Nicholson negotiated a very tough deal, not only earning himself a hefty fee and box office percentage, but his scenes were all to be filmed within a three-week period. That didn't quite happen in practice, and to further compound matters the British Exchequer withheld a sizeable chunk of his salary in 'withholding tax' which greatly upset Jack; he vowed never to work in the UK again.

Sean Young was cast as the female lead Vicki Vale and as her role involved riding a horse, we arranged for her to take lessons near the studio. Then one day I received a call saying Sean had fallen from the horse, and couldn't move her shoulder. The studio doctor attended to her but said she should see a specialist in London and have X-rays taken. I asked the Line Producer to accompany her as a) she was in pain and needed someone with her, and b) I needed to know what the bottom line was in terms of whether she would be able to film.

"I can't," he said. "I'm going out to dinner tonight."

There are certain things I think are more important than social gatherings, and this was one of them! So I said I'd accompany her.

We met the specialist and he examined her shoulder and said it was a nasty break and would take some time to mend.

"How long before she can move around?" I asked.

"At least three to four weeks, minimum," he replied.

**Michael Keaton as the Caped Crusader**

We were due to start shooting on her the next week, and this was to be her big starring break. My heart sank. I told Sean I'd have to speak to the insurers and Terry Semel in LA. I knew they'd likely agree our only option would be to re-cast, and I of course would have to be the one to break it to Sean that she would be off the movie.

Meanwhile we needed a star who was not only good casting, but available to start on the following Monday - it was now Tuesday! That wasn't likely.

The insurance company came in to see me the next morning, and asked outright, "How much is this going to cost us?" They knew they were facing a potentially huge multi-million dollar claim, as the production looked as though it would have to be halted until a replacement was found. Having been in similar situations with Stanley Kubrick, I knew if we made a full claim we faced weeks of disruption, mounds of paperwork and more headaches then anyone could stand. It would also mean future premiums on Warner's productions would go through the roof, as they did with Kubrick. In fact Stanley never knew how much the policies cost us on one of his films; because of his history they were huge!

So I made the insurers a proposal: obviously we were all keen shooting continued as planned, and I felt reasonably confident we'd find a replacement actress given the calibre of the production, so I suggested we'd settle for a lump sum payment of $2 million for losing our leading lady. Although it sounds a huge sum, it was actually much less than the cost of halting production until we re-cast.

I called Terry Semel.

"This has never been done before Paul, what are the risks to us?"

"If we can get a new star on set by Tuesday, then we're in profit," I replied.

"And if we can't?"

"Then it starts costing us," I said.

Producer Jon Peters suggested Kim Basinger and on checking with her agent, she was available and willing to start immediately (obviously for the right price), and sure enough she was on set the following Monday. Everyone breathed a sigh of relief, and we made a few quid from the deal.

Months and months later I was in LA and an executive in Warner's Production Department invited me to lunch with the insurers we used on our films. He beamed widely, and told me they were in to present him with a $2 million cheque. It was the *Batman* $2 million. Now, he must have known I'd done that deal but immediately after lunch - and without referring to me at all - he went to see Terry Semel and handed over the cheque which he said he had negotiated for. I've never been one to seek praise, but I certainly don't like anyone else taking the credit due to me.

Back to the film. Production designer Anton Furst was the man responsible for the gloomy, Gothic look of Gotham City, which was built in its entirety on the Pinewood backlot. It was truly impressive and worlds away from the camp 1960s TV series. Working flat out with his 14-strong depart-

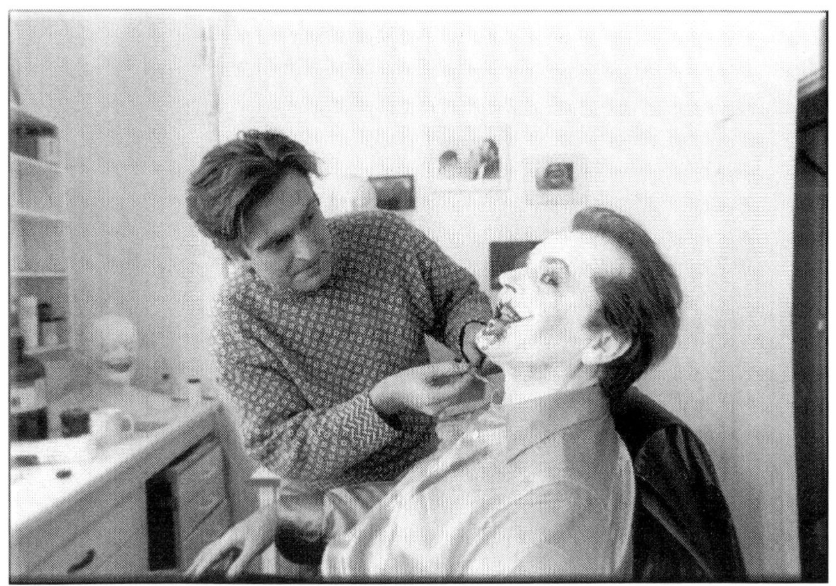

**Jack Nicholson, here in make up, stole the picture in my opinion!**

ment and a construction team of 200, it took only five months to build.

There were four stages of construction. The buildings were first supported by scaffolding and clad in plywood. Then a plaster, or sometimes fibreglass, covering was added and finally painted. With a main street which was a quarter of a mile long, I was told that it was the biggest set on the lot since *Cleopatra.* It was certainly a massive challenge, as Anton didn't have the security of shooting on stages in controlled conditions. Plus without the stage rigging to help secure lights from, massive cranes were brought into service.

The cathedral was the setting for Batman's final battle with the Joker and was one of the major buildings in the city. Filming in and around the cathedral was very complicated, and a number of different methods were employed to create the necessary effect. On the lot and in the studio, full-size set pieces were built to represent the top and bottom of the building, with gigantic bells. Two other scales were used to construct the length in between.

We used a lot of Pinewood in the film, not least the restaurant for Billy Dee Williams' political campaign speech.

**On set, on the Pinewood backlot**

With *Batman*, director Tim Burton heralded the arrival of a new kind of blockbuster. Pinewood was participating in the birth of the 'event' movie.

I enjoyed working on the film immensely, though there was one incident when I felt terribly undermined, and it was no fault of the production, but rather Warner Bros.

We were running slightly behind schedule and I was pressuring Tim, in the nicest way possible, to try and get it in the can. Warner Bros.' Mark Canton meanwhile, who was great friends with the producer Jon Peters, called our line producer - who had taped the call - and said, "don't worry, if you need an extra day then take an extra day."

I had a go at Terry Semel and said, "This is not on. If he wants to have a go at me for pressuring Tim then he needs to speak to me directly and not go behind my back." But that, as I've said before, is indicative of management - they like to be friends with the star players and never have to give them bad news.

Happily, when we screened the finished film we knew we had something special and very unique on our hands, and I remember saying to Terry Semel that we should change the title.

"What do you mean?" he asked.

"I think it should be called *The Joker* because when you see it Terry, you'll no doubt agree just how brilliant Jack Nicholson is, and how he steals the film from everyone else."

After seeing the cut, Terry asked Tim Burton, "How much more material is there that's not in the film?"

Tim looked a little perplexed and replied, "That is the film. There might be five or ten minutes left in the cutting room, but pretty much everything we shot is there on the screen."

Unlike other directors, Tim only shot what he needed to. He was always economical, and I greatly admired him for that. I remember when we shot *Mission: Impossible II* we had over three hours of film, that had to be trimmed down to two; similarly on a film called *Fred Claus* we had a film initially running over three hours. I did tell everyone they were shooting too much, to no avail, and so when it was cut down to two hours a lot of money had been needlessly spent.

We all knew we had a hit on our hands so fully expected a sequel to be moved into production with Keaton, and accordingly I went to see Pinewood's MD Cyril Howard to negotiate a deal to keep the Gotham City set on the Pinewood backlot. With maintenance, scaffolding hire and security it wasn't a cheap proposition, costing in the region of $250,000, but long-term would obviously save Warner's a lot of money when the sequel swung into action in May 1990.

Unlike a lot of producers today, I never booked stage space until I knew I needed it. Yes, I'd pencil in requirements and maybe pay a small deposit if I had to, but I never block-booked huge quantities of stages which, in this instance, was just as well. You see Tim was given more creative control on the second film, *Batman Returns*, and Michael Keaton received a hefty pay rise and said that he "didn't want to work in the UK again" as part of the conditions laid down in his contract, which Tim agreed to. So, sadly for me, it was decided to shoot in California and I had to make the call to scrap the Gotham sets at Pinewood. The studio was not particularly busy at the time, and had lost the latest James Bond film to Mexico, so this news was quite a blow to Pinewood and the British film industry as a whole.

an adventure in obsession...
CLINT EASTWOOD
WHITE HUNTER
BLACK HEART
WARNER BROS. PRESENTS
PRODUCED AND DIRECTED BY CLINT EASTWOOD

# 1990

## *White Hunter Black Heart*

Clint Eastwood directed and starred in this African-set film, which was based on film director John Huston's obsession with shooting an elephant during his filming of *An African Queen.*

I helped set up the film in London and Zimbabwe, and after a recce in Africa with Production Designer John Graysmark I sent loads of pictures back to Clint with various suggestions. Although Clint takes an active interest in every aspect of his films, if he feels he can trust you then he just lets you get on with the job - as he did in this instance. He never came to Zimbabwe with us, nor to London for the casting session with Mary Selway. Mary made her suggestions, put people on tape and sent them to Clint, who would make his comments known back to Mary.

Clint wasn't even going to come into London before we were to ship off to Africa, as he wanted to go to Paris to buy a helicopter. Once there he phoned me and suggested that as he had the Warner jet, I fly to Harare with him, from Paris. Jeff Fahey, Clint's co-star, was on board also, and was a thoroughly nice man to work with too.

On arriving in Harare, we all had to attend a reception President Mugabe was holding in Clint's honour, and I have to say it wasn't a very pleasant experience meeting that man but with that out of the way we next flew up to

**On the buses! The shuttle at Luxor airport with Jeff Fahey, Clint's stand-in and his publicist Joe Hyams**

**Setting up a crane shot at Northolt Airport**

Lake Kariba where we were to start production. Bearing in mind Clint had never been there before, I'd taken the decision to take the morning to show Clint the planned locations, and in the afternoon thought we'd have a few drinks with the cast and crew.

"That's a waste of a day," Clint said.

"Come on Clint!" I laughed, "One day's prep on a film like this isn't so bad."

But that was Clint, he couldn't bear to think we were 'wasting' valuable time. Mind you that isn't to say he'd work flat out all day long, as quite often if he felt he'd done all he wanted and was on schedule, around 4pm he'd say, "The light's gone guys, let's wrap it up for today", and of course we'd be standing there in blistering sunshine. But that was his way of saying "Let's go home early".

Anyhow, back to Lake Kariba, the next day we started shooting and bang on schedule we finished a few weeks later and returned to Pinewood for studio shots; again it was an absolute pleasure working with Clint, though that isn't to say he suffers fools - if anyone messes up or can't do their job, then he wants them out of the way, but do a good job and he's your friend for life and you'll work with him year after year.

Clint never stops working either, though I know the insurance companies aren't keen for him to act and direct in the same movie any more, and I put it down to him knowing the value a picture has. Yes he wants to find good stories and make good films, but he does it with an eye on commerciality. If he wants to make a film like *Birdie* for instance, he knows the widespread cinema audiences won't flock to see a movie about a jazz musician much as they would a *Dirty Harry* film, so he knows he has to make it 'for a price' to ensure it makes a return. He always does.

The thing I like most about Clint is that he treats making a film as a job of work. It's all very matter of fact with him. Recently, for example, I heard about a film setting up at Pinewood and the caterer was presented with a list of special meals for the actors, director, producer and line producer. Clint on the other hand, at lunchtime, would walk over to the catering truck, go inside, lift up the lids and ask, "And what's this... and this... and this?"

**Me, on location. David Puttnam is directly behind me with a cap on.**

"Irish stew," might be one reply.

Clint will then walk back out and join the queue with everyone else, and then at the counter say, "I'll take the Irish stew." He'd then happily sit next to anyone from the electricians to carpenters to leading actors and eat his lunch. A short while afterwards he'd be back on the stage ready to start work again.

My grandson, in 2010, was an Assistant Director, worked on *Hereafter* with Clint. He told me the runner went over to Clint one morning and said, "Mr. Eastwood, here's the menu. What would you like for lunch?" - this now obviously being the normal procedure in film-making.

"Why are you giving this to me now?" Clint asked.

"I'll go and get it for you and bring it over at lunchtime."

"I'm quite capable of walking over to get my own meal," Clint said, and turned around to carry on working. It's so refreshing to hear stories like that!

I'd happily say that if I'd only ever made Clint Eastwood movies in my career, then I don't think I'd ever have retired.

**Clint Eastwood on location in Zimbabwe**

## *Memphis Belle*

Producer David Puttnam had a first-look deal with Warner Bros. and brought *Memphis Belle* to us as being a film he really, really wanted to make. It was a World War II story set on a 1943 American Airbase in the UK, and centred on the crew of the infamous Memphis Belle and their completing twenty-five missions.

David had secured a deal with the relatively new 'British Sky Broadcasting' company (which was later bought out by SKY) and also with Natwest Bank, who were dipping their toes in film-financing with him.

It was a terrific production to work on because whilst it was very demanding in terms of bringing in real B-17 bombers and choreographing all the aerial action, everything ran like clockwork.

One thing I learned from working with Clint Eastwood on *Firefox* is that there is nothing particularly thrilling about seeing three people sitting in the cockpit of a plane, unless of course something very exciting is happening such as them coming under fire, or suchlike. So I discussed this with David and his director Michael Caton-Jones and we agreed to try and keep those 'ordinary' scenes in the cockpit to a minimum.

Of course with their flying helmets on, as again was the problem with Clint, you don't see much of the actors' faces and that's what the audience wants to see; so we were very mindful of that.

**On location at Northolt Airport, near Pinewood Studios, with my two grandsons**

**On location with producer David Puttnam**

**Watch your heads. A flypast on the airfield.**

**The cast of Memphis Belle**

In Gdansk with Mark Canton of Warner Bros.
and the team to meet President Wałęsa

# 1991

## *Lech Wałęsa - the film that never was*

One of the most, shall we say, unusual projects I was asked to set up was when I heard Warner's had done a deal to make a film of the life story of the first elected Polish President - who was instrumental in the country emerging from Communist rule - Lech Wałęsa.

Mr. Wałęsa arrived in London and I was asked to meet him, and take along the agreement (and cheque) with the idea of us all meeting up at a later date to decide what part of his life the script would concentrate on.

A couple of weeks later, I received a call from Mark Canton, President of the Film Division at Warner's, telling me he was flying in on the company jet and wanted to pick me up to travel with him to Gdansk to meet the President. On board, Mark had his creative assistant with him and two Canadian producers, who were not Warner people, but obviously had an interest in the project, and the studio's head of publicity.

I tried to phone ahead to Gdansk airport and arrange for some cars to meet us and drive us to the Solidarity offices, but it proved impossible so I realised I'd have to do it on arrival. On touchdown, I was just about to get out of my seat to meet the ground staff when the Captain said, "Oh Paul, we need to get the boxes out of the hold."

"What boxes?" I asked.

Mark added, "I've brought Lech some Looney Tunes toys as gifts."

The boxes, I'm not kidding you, were the size of six large filing cabinets. Faced with having to find transport for us and them, I was trying to find someone who spoke English - to no avail - and in the end I found a porter to load up the boxes. It was now noon, and we were due in the President's office so you can imagine I wasn't best pleased that we were still farting around at the airport with Looney Tunes toys; then the customs officers started asking questions and wouldn't let us through, so I gave them two of the boxes. I explained what they were, and they ultimately seemed quite happy with their new cuddly toys and let us pass through with the remaining four boxes. But could we fit them in a car? Could we heck.

I eventually managed to find an old boy with a truck, and through a series of hand gestures, writing and offering him a bit of money, he loaded up the boxes and agreed to follow us.

On arriving at the Solidarity offices, the President's PA said we were late and that he was unable to see us. She explained he never saw anybody who was late as it then made him late for subsequent appointments. "Let's look at a meeting on another day," she said.

I explained that my colleagues had flown in from California, and it wasn't really possible.

"Would you please tell Mr. Wałęsa that I'm the gentleman who met him in London, and helped with the paperwork." I didn't want to say, "I'm the bloke who gave him the big cheque" as I'm not sure it was supposed to be public knowledge within the Solidarity party then, but I felt sure the President would get my drift.

Sure enough he said he could spare a short time.

The President greeted us, wearing a pair of old jeans and what looked like carpet slippers, and we started talking about the film.

After about ten minutes he said, "I don't know why you want to make a film about me, as my life is very boring. I was an electrician who organised strikes, meetings and rallies to get rid of Communism. There was no violence, no sex and nothing very exciting. There is no scandal."

Mark Canton leapt up and said, "Lech! Lech! You'll love what we're going to do; it will be just like *Driving Miss Daisy*."

The President stared blankly. He'd not heard of *Lawrence Of Arabia* so he certainly wasn't going to be familiar with *Driving Miss Daisy*!

"About the old lady and her driver," Mark continued, "you'd think that didn't look interesting on paper but it was one of our biggest grossing movies. And that's what I'm going to do with this film."

"I just don't know how you'd do that," the President replied, "it would make an interesting documentary maybe?"

Anyhow, we thanked him for his time and left. The plane stopped in Paris as Mark Canton wanted to do some shopping, and I then headed back to London never to hear another word about the film. The money, of course, was all written off. Was I surprised?

**The President was happy to see us!**

In my office at Pinewood. This chair was given to me by Bud Ornstein from which he'd made deals on Bond, the Beatles and many other big movies.

# 1992

## *Leaving Warner's*

I had been with Warner Bros. since 1969 so had enjoyed twenty-three years with the company by 1992. I was approaching my 60th birthday, and although I still had two years to run on my current contract, I remember driving home one night and thinking, "I really don't want to do this anymore." I wasn't enjoying my job as much as I used to, and thought perhaps it was time to call it a day. I was slightly frustrated with the state of the UK film industry at that time too, as it was undoubtedly one of the quietest and most depressing periods ever. There had been just three films shooting at Pinewood, along with some TV dramas and the Conservative Administration of the time had little to no interest in supporting British films.

Seven years earlier in 1985 the Eady Levy - which had been responsible for bringing so many films and filmmakers to Britain - had been abolished, and Margaret Thatcher's policy of businesses either sustaining themselves or sinking was rigid. Whilst other European countries, most notably France, had subsidies for film, and Ireland was just about to launch an amazingly successful tax credit (Section 35), Thatcher was not interested in the economic and cultural benefits movies could offer the UK.

So, not surprisingly, Warner's activity in Britain was nowhere near as busy as it used to be and I became less and less directly involved in what I loved doing - making films.

When I arrived home I told my wife, and she said it was my decision to make but cautioned me, "I know you. You can't just retire at 60, because you'll go mad."

The next day I rang Terry Semel's assistant Judith and asked if I could fly over to see Terry, and she gave me some dates for the following week. When I arrived at his Burbank office I told him exactly what I'd told my wife the week before.

"I've done the job for so long Terry, that now I'm not enjoying it I know it's no good for me nor the company to keep going and it's time to pack it up."

He was quite surprised and asked if I'd received an offer from someone else. I told him no, I just wanted to leave at the time of my 60th birthday the following February. He agreed, but on condition I stay on as a consultant and see out my contract, which was fair enough. He also asked if I wanted a production deal, which with hindsight perhaps I should have accepted, but again I said no, I just wanted to bow out.

"Maybe in time Terry, if you want me to work on a movie," I added, "then perhaps I will. But right now I want a clean break."

After a year had passed I realised the worst job you can ever have is a consultancy role; the people coming into the position you've left don't want to hear how you would have done things and you get so frustrated in not having any control or authority that it's a bit of a pointless and thankless job.

I'd moved out of the Warner Bros. bungalow (out of their hair) and into a new office in Pinewood's main administration building. I must admit to wondering quite what I'd do after my two-year consultancy was over - though I never for one minute regretted making the decision to leave Warner's.

My retirement party (1992) with Rick Senat in Pinewood's Ballroom

SEAN CONNERY • RICHARD GERE
JULIA ORMOND
Their greatest battle would be for her love.
FIRST KNIGHT
COLUMBIA PICTURES PRESENTS
SEAN CONNERY RICHARD GERE JULIA ORMOND "FIRST KNIGHT" BEN CROSS
JERRY GOLDSMITH GIL NETTER ERIC RATTRAY JANET ZUCKER
WALTER MURCH, A.C.E. JOHN BOX ADAM GREENBERG, A.S.C.
LORNE CAMERON & DAVID HOSELTON AND WILLIAM NICHOLSON
WILLIAM NICHOLSON JERRY ZUCKER HUNT LOWRY JERRY ZUCKER

# 1994-1995

## *First Knight*

Just as my two-year consultancy period was ending with Warner's, Gary Martin, who was head of Production for Sony-Columbia phoned me up, told me he had a problem on *First Knight* and asked if I was free to, and interested in, taking it over for him.

It seemed I was now an independent producer - and one for hire!

It was a big-budget feature shooting at Pinewood and was all about the King Arthur and Camelot legend, starring Sean Connery and Richard Gere with an all-star supporting cast.

They'd been in production a few weeks at this point, so I met with Gary, Eric Rattray the Line Producer and Jerry Zucker the director to get a feel for everything, and the problems they'd been having.

"We're way, way over budget," Gary told me, "and Jerry is dropping behind schedule; I need to bring things back on track. To try and control the cost of the sets we've fired John Box."

"You've fired John Box because the sets are over budget? That's not right. If anyone needs John Box on this picture you do, but the secret with John is for him to have an Art Director and Construction Manager who know how to manage their costs. John could design you the best garden shed in the world, but if you asked him how much it cost to build he'd have no idea, and say, 'Oh, it shouldn't be that much.'"

"You feel strongly about him?" Gary asked.

"Yes, I think you should reinstate him."

I'd known John, and respected him hugely, for more years than I could remember and I understood his whole approach to a project. Thankfully they agreed and John returned to join us.

I looked at the budget and schedule, we agreed on a plan, and stuck to it.

Jerry Zucker, up until this time, had only ever really directed comedy films and was famous for the likes of *The Naked Gun* movies. *First Knight* was a very serious drama, with lots of action and complicated dialogue. It's no wonder he felt a little bit out of his depth on the schedule they'd given him initially, plus he had the complicated issues of having two huge and quite demanding stars heading his cast. The costume designer, who was integral to the look of this period story, was an Italian lady who was wonderfully talented but had never, ever been on a film of this size and scope. This was a different world for them both.

The producer was an American chap, and I remember a few weeks into the film my assistant Lidia called me and said, "Sean wants to see you in his dressing room." I'd known Sean from my early days at Pinewood when he was making films like *Hell Drivers* there so we had a little bit of history behind us, which I've always found useful in this business.

"Come in Paul and shut the f-ing door," he said when I arrived at his dressing room.

"I'm only going to tell you this once Paul," he said - I have the greatest respect for Sean because he is the consummate professional but he doesn't suffer fools – "I am not going on set anymore if that producer is there."

"What do you mean?" I asked.

"If he wants to go on set when I'm not, and it's just Gere, fine but if he walks on and I'm on set then that's it, I'm going home."

The American chap was a perfectly pleasant man, though admittedly not a man I'd allow to run a bath, but I couldn't understand what he'd done to upset Sean so much.

"Every time he comes on set he sits next to me and is on the bloody

**A medieval village set designed by John Box in the Pinewood Gardens**

**Another John Box set, built around the fruit orchard at Pinewood**

phone to his wife. He wanders in at 10.30am after all the decisions have been made first thing, and all he does is talk about his f-ing dinner arrangements on the phone. 'Get the chateaubriand, get the Chateau Neuf du Pape wine'... I'm trying to concentrate and learn this difficult dialogue. Please tell him to keep away."

Sean then looked me straight in the eyes and added, "Otherwise I won't be there Paul."

My first reaction was that really the studio, Columbia, should relay this to the producer, as after all they were employing him to run the picture, but then I thought they might take time in doing so, with the time difference in LA, so Lidia asked him to come over to my office.

"He says why don't you come over to the set?" my assistant relayed to me.

My facial expression said it all.

"No, Paul says this is very important, you HAVE to come to the office," Lidia told him firmly.

When he arrived, I told him bluntly. "Sean asked me to go and see him and told me, under no circumstances will he go on the set if you're there."

"What are you talking about?"

"He's told me categorically he won't work if you're there!"

The producer walked over to me, put his arm around my shoulder and said, "But Paul, I absolutely love Sean."

"I know you do," I said, but sensing I needed to be even more blunt, added, "but he really doesn't like you."

There was silence for a moment before he asked "What's the problem?"

"He says you don't concentrate on what's happening on set, you're more interested in your private life."

"Well I shall go and talk to Sean..." he replied.

"I really do not think that is a good idea. Personally, if I were you, I'd leave it, keep away for a while and I'm sure over time it will smooth out."

He reluctantly agreed, nodded and left my office. Sean had been living outside of Britain for many years as a tax exile, and he was only allowed to spend a certain number of days (or rather nights, as it was then) in the coun-

**Sean Connery and Richard Gere on the Camelot Castle set on Pinewood's backlot**

try before all his annual income would fall subject to UK tax. Therefore, we had to schedule his scenes in order he could leave late Friday afternoons and fly to Spain, and return on Monday mornings.

His son, Jason, was then making a *Harry Palmer* film in Russia for producer Harry Alan Towers and, in the days before mobile phones were all the rage, it wasn't easy getting hold of him; I could see Sean was becoming a little concerned, so I suggested my assistant Lidia, who spoke Russian, might be able to help; sure enough she got them together on the telephone, and Sean came over to thank me.

"When's he coming home?" I asked. "Is he going to stay with you?"

"Staying with me?!" Sean exclaimed. "We don't have enough room."

"But you've got the flat in Eaton Square," I replied, knowing that all the properties are rather swish in that area.

"We only have one bedroom, so people can't stay."

That really summed up the 'careful' approach Sean has always had towards money. And who needs to fritter it away on house guests?!

One of the only slight problems we had on the film, meanwhile, was good weather. I know it sounds ironic, when we are always hoping for fine conditions shooting a film outdoors, but the problem lay in the fact that Camelot Castle - which we'd constructed on the Pinewood backlot - had nothing but pure blue skies surrounding it throughout October 1994, so much so it looked like we'd erected a large blue screen behind the set, and as a result it looked quite false, though everything else was real, including the bread, spit-roasted animals, and fires on set. We built part of a village in the Pinewood orchard and also transformed the outdoor paddock tank with a section of Camelot Castle on it, in order Richard Gere (or rather his stunt double) could dive from a tower and into the moat... or at least appear that way.

The sword fighting was all CGI. While the actors held hilts of swords in their hands, all the blades were added in later. It was a very exciting use of the new technology and one that doubtlessly pleased the health and safety officer, but looking back at the film now you can see the joins as the technology was not quite as advanced as today.

Location work was completed in North Wales, in the slate quarries, and we were one of the first big films to shoot there in many years. Buoyed by the investment we made in the local economy, the council decided to maintain a full-time film officer, Huw Edwin Jones, who went on to attract many more blockbusters to the area.

I don't think it set the world on fire in terms of critical or box office acclaim, but it's a fairly good film which I'm pleased to say came in on schedule and budget, and as it was my first as an 'independent producer', I'd like to think it stood me well for future assignments; but because I was used to working at Warner Bros. where you were never allowed to take a credit - the only exception being *Firefox* with Clint Eastwood, who had insisted - I didn't worry about it as I thought people would know what I'd done.

Of course these days, with the internet being the be-all and end all of everything, I'm not listed as Executive Producer for *First Knight* on the various sites and consequently I wonder if perhaps I missed out further along the line. Not that I'm worried now!

TOM CRUISE

MISSION: IMPOSSIBLE

MAY 22

# 1995

## *Village Roadshow*

Terry Semel called me one day and asked if I would fly to Brisbane, on behalf of Warner Bros., to check out the Village Roadshow Studios (and production company) as WB were thinking about buying into the company. The idea was also to extend into a production deal whereby the parties co-financed films and each took certain territories for distribution.

I flew to meet the studio management in Brisbane - Mr. Kirby and his sons - and was very impressed with the set-up and its team; after spending time there I flew back, via LA, and stopped off to see Terry to give him my report and recommendation that it would indeed be a good deal to make.

That's how the 'Warner-Village Roadshow' collaboration started, and in 1997 they co-financed their first film together - *Practical Magic* with Sandra Bullock and Nicole Kidman, swiftly followed by *Analyze This* and *The Matrix.*

I was invited to a dinner, which was to celebrate the consummation of the company marriage, and Mr. Kirby leaned across the table to cut my tie off with a pair of scissors.

"This is a custom we have," he explained, as I sat looking at the remains of my very expensive new tie. He handed me the scissors and told me to do similar to his. In retrospect it was a lovely gesture, but that taught me a valuable lesson - buy a cheap tie if you ever do a deal with Australians.

Bruce Berman, the now current head of Village Roadshow, was formerly a production executive at Warner's and they've kept extending their deal; it's now running through to 2017, and I believe has produced over seventy films, so far, and even a UK cinema chain at one point before selling it to Vue Cinemas.

## *Mission: Impossible*

Fred Gallo, head of production at Paramount, called me up and said:

"We've got this film called *Mission: Impossible* that we've done some preliminary work on, and are setting up at Pinewood; we will be changing the people we have on it though. Tom Cruise is starring and producing, and I'd like you to meet him."

It sounded interesting!

I knew they had offices downstairs from mine at Pinewood, but I couldn't go to see Paula Wagner - Tom's business partner - there, as they hadn't yet told the people they were firing that they had been fired. So I met Paula in a London hotel, and then I met Tom. We had a chat and they explained their man would be leaving, though there wasn't any bad blood, and I agreed to come on board.

Paula was very much a creative sort of producer, in that she liked working on the development and preparation of a project and that was where her strengths lay. Tom was the sort of producer who was always interested in everything, but without wanting to get into the nitty-gritty of everyday matters; he liked to know everything was running to schedule but as he had scripts to learn, action scenes to choreograph, 'the look' of his character to think about with the costume department, he didn't have time for much else so appointed a man named Michael Doven as Associate Producer, who used to double-check on things with me. Tom was the star, as well as producer, but he treated everyone with great respect and was always approachable and friendly.

The bulk of the location work was to be done in Prague, and set at night,

**Tom, myself, Paula Wagner and Associate Producer Michael Doven**

so I had to meet the local Mayor to gain all the various permissions. There was no doubt in anyone's mind that this was going to be a huge production.

"What will it be like when they all arrive?" he asked warily.

"To be honest, it'll be just like the Russian invasion," I replied.

He thought I was joking...

With it being mainly night shoots we had to light three square miles of the city, and had more generators, lights, trucks and cables than you've ever seen in your life. In fact all the tourists were saying, "Prague look so beautiful at night" - they thought it was usual to have everything from the castle to the cathedral and town squares all illuminated brightly!

As Prague offered various financial incentives to attract filmmakers, one of the requirements necessary to qualify was that we had to engage a local production company and crew to assist on that part of the shoot. That was all fine, and par for the course. Well, that is to say apart from the fact that my predecessor engaged a local company that had only ever been involved in small, local films before. They were immediately out of their depth, but they had a signed contract... and to top things Paramount - us! - were not even

**Tom and Jon Voight rehearsing on the 007 stage (channel tunnel) set.**

**The 'burst' of the restaurant window was shot at Pinewood**

signatories to the bank account there, and had no control at all.

Director Brian De Palma had selected a number of Government buildings by the river, and was quite adamant they were the ones we'd film - rightly so too as they looked very good, but we kept receiving huge facility bills, and each week another would arrive for far more than the previous one. With us shooting nights, I had to sleep during the day so consequently didn't have much time to challenge the bills with the issuing authorities as it was always difficult to get to meetings.

My assistant Lidia told me that I would have to get a meeting with the (late) Czech President Havel. It sounds fantastical, but Lidia - I have come to realise - always knows someone who knows someone else... and sure enough she got us in to see the President.

"But we have to ask Tom to come too," she cautioned - knowing full well how much weight that would swing our way.

Tom, Paula, Lidia and I explained that we were thoroughly enjoying filming in the city, and how it was looking magnificent on the big screen, but then explained about the bills the Ministry was sending in each week.

President Havel said, "I'm delighted you're enjoying yourselves here, but there really isn't a lot I can do."

"But you are the President," Lidia said.

He agreed to talk to his Prime Minister; soon afterwards things got back under control financially and it all ran smoothly.

Returning to Pinewood, we had to film the climax of the story, which concerns a train going into the Channel Tunnel with our hero on top. I called a meeting with Eurostar, who just didn't want to know - they were not remotely interested in cooperating. Feeling we were facing a bit of a problem, I flew to Paris to meet the Sales & Marketing Executive at TGV whom I knew and he was wonderful, as he immediately saw the PR opportunities of Tom Cruise, a big Hollywood film and so on, and willingly arranged for us to have all the trains and rolling stock we needed.

We constructed a huge tunnel and train set on the 007 Stage at Pinewood, and to achieve the effect of Tom clinging on to the roof of a fast-mov-

**Tom Cruise hanging around on set, with stunt coordinator Greg Powell**

ing train, brought in loads and loads of wind machines and when you think they were essentially aeroplane engines, you can imagine just how powerful they were. Tom wanted to, and does do, most of his own stunts and did not want any safety wires.

"Tom, you can't stand on top of the train with those wind machines on!" I reasoned, concerned we'd never get insurance cover for him to do it in any event.

"Well what'll happen if I don't wear the wires?" he asked.

"You'll be at Shepperton and we'll be at Pinewood!" I answered.

It was a really tough scene to film and although it was mainly set against green screen the force of the 140 mph wind hitting Tom distorted his face, pushed him off balance and was physically a hugely demanding sequence - his fitness and stamina were enviable! The wires did indeed save Tom from being catapulted through the stage's roof, and of course they were 'painted out' in post-production so nobody would have known they'd been there.

Tom would always do as much as he could and I remember that the scene that takes place in a glass-walled restaurant in Prague, with a big lobster tank in the middle and three huge fish tanks overhead, was his idea. There were sixteen tonnes of water in the tanks and there was some concern that when they detonated, a lot of glass would fly around. So much so, director Brian De Palma tried the sequence with a stuntman, but felt it didn't look convincing so asked Tom to do it, and despite the possibility that he could have drowned, Tom readily agreed.

The film was so full of terrific and stylish scenes, and everyone remembers the sequence where Tom infiltrates a vault, drops down from a rope horizontally and hangs just inches above his target. As I said before, his fitness and stamina were enviable. He really reinvented the action movie!

Key to the film's success, I believe, was Tom's selection of Brian De Palma as director. Up until that time, De Palma had made fairly dramatic films such as *Carlito's Way, Scarface* and *The Untouchables*. This was a whole new genre to him really, and Tom saw that as a strength, as he wanted a director who would bring thought and dramatic tension to the movie, not just supervise a series of chase and fight scenes.

I got on very well with Brian, and he was certainly a man of few words. I remember before we started shooting, the studio insisted that the budget and schedule was signed off not only by Cruise, Wagner, myself and our accountant Mike Smith, but by the director too. However, the one signature missing as we moved into production was Brian's.

I approached him on the stage one day. "Brian, I'm sorry to raise it but I'm being really beaten up by the studio over getting you to sign off the schedule and budget."

"Where is it?" he asked.

"It's with your assistant in the office."

"OK," he said.

A couple of days went by and he still hadn't signed the paperwork.

On set, I approached him again. "Brian, I know you have more important things to worry about than this, but is there a problem with the schedule or budget that you don't want to commit to?"

"No. I don't want to sign it," he replied.

"Can I ask why?" I asked, in growing frustration.

"The reason I won't sign it Paul is because Paramount have not signed my contract, so why should I sign this?"

I returned the paperwork to Paramount, told them the reasons and it went unsigned.

In any other business, contracts would always be signed before a job commences - but not in movies!

Brian was always on set early, and worked bloody hard, but when we broke for lunch around 1pm I knew we wouldn't see him back on set until around 3pm, because he used to like to have a little rest. Quite often we'd run through quite late into the evenings, so I could understand why he liked a break, and he worked much the better for it. One lunchtime though, Tom wanted to get something or other underway earlier, and went looking for Brian.

"Mr. De Palma is having a lie down and will be ready at 3pm," his assistant said.

Tom was about to argue, and I stepped in to say, "Tom, it's the same

**Director Brian DePalma on set**

every day. This is how he works, we'll just have to wait."

The final shot of the movie was to be filmed on a Tuesday, at Heathrow Airport, where Tom's character says goodbye to Ving Rhames and the film ends. On the Sunday evening prior, Brian called me at home.

"Paul, I don't want to shoot at Heathrow on Tuesday."

"Why not, Brian?"

"It doesn't work, it doesn't work for me," he replied.

"But we film on Tuesday... what is it you're looking to do instead?"

"I want to shoot in the courtyard of a pub overlooking St. Paul's Cathedral."

The conversation ended with me thinking, "How the hell are we going to pull this one off in twenty-four hours?", so I called Chris Brock - our location manager - and a couple of others, and they tore about on Monday, but by the evening we were able to take Brian to see a pub that they'd found and he said he was "very happy".

I'd meanwhile been given the name of the owner, Lord somebody or other, who lived in Manchester. I called him at home, and after apologising for the late-evening intrusion explained, "I'm Paul Hitchcock from Paramount Pictures, and we are producing a film called *Mission: Impossible* with Tom Cruise, and I'm a very desperate man."

"Mr. Hitchcock," he replied, "nothing gives me more pleasure than talking to a desperate man."

"Oh," I said.

"Because there is no room for negotiation!" he added.

I reached an agreement and with a small crew, we filmed right in the centre of the City of London the next morning and Brian was very appreciative.

Incidentally, a couple of years later, MGM called me and said they were going to make a film with Brian De Palma called *Nazi Gold* which, as the title suggests, was all about the gold snaffled away by Hitler into Swiss Banks - and this was about the raid to reclaim it, a bit like *The Monuments Men* premise.

"Would you be interested?" they asked.

I thought it sounded fun, and so they suggested I give Brian a call to discuss it all.

"I'll send you the script," he said, ever a man of few words.

"Well, would it be okay for me to work on the film with you?" I ventured to ask, not sure how I should read his reply.

"Yes, sure," he answered. "Read the script and just move on, looking for locations."

"Shouldn't we meet though?" I asked.

"Paul. You know what I look like, and I know what you look like. Why do we need to meet?"

I went over to see the production people at MGM, and they told me they wanted to start in the summer and I should head off to Zurich and Geneva post-haste, which is exactly what I did; along the way I kept sending ideas and reports back to Brian in New York.

I spent around three weeks in Switzerland, and must admit I was met rather frostily by all the Swiss Banks I approached as they operated under tight veils of secrecy of course, but eventually I made some headway; however I felt it quite strange that I hadn't heard anything back from Brian.

When I called the MGM office, they told me, "Oh, he resigned from the picture a week ago."

"But I've been traipsing around Europe and have just sent him another bundle of papers and photos," I said, feeling rather exasperated.

I never heard another word from Brian, until another film came along nearly ten years later - *The Black Dahlia* - for which independent finance had been raised on a relatively modest budget, away from the studio system which he was seemingly rallying against. But I didn't think it was a project that would work, for me at least, on the budget and timescale they had in mind, so I declined.

Personally, I think the first *Mission* was the best of all the *Mission: Impossible* films as it had a terrific, if slightly convoluted storyline, with good characters and believable action. In fact I remember being at the premiere in London, and standing in the foyer of the Odeon Leicester Square I saw two ladies coming out of the loo; the first one said, "I really enjoyed that, but what was it about?"

The second said, "I've no idea, but wasn't it good?"

WHO IS THE SAINT

# 1996-1997

## *The Saint*

In the 1960s Roger Moore had played Simon Templar in the long-running TV series of *The Saint* and then in the 1970s Ian Ogilvy took over the halo for a couple of years, before Simon Dutton had a go in the ill-fated 1980s series.

Roger Moore and his producing partner Bob Baker had bought the rights to the character from Leslie Charteris, and the studios courted them about making a feature film. I believe it started out as a *Son Of The Saint* premise with Roger reprising his role as (now) ageing Simon Templar who discovers an illegitimate son who eventually takes over the halo.

Paramount sealed a deal and hired Robert Evans as producer, Stephen Zaillian as producer and Sydney Pollack as director. Ralph Fiennes was tipped to star. I saw Bob Evans in the car park at Pinewood and despite the many intervening years since we last met, he said, "The kid's still in the picture then?" when he saw me.

Soon afterwards Bob left the film (though still gets a credit), followed by the writer and director! David Brown replaced Bob and brought in Philip Noyce as the new director, along with Val Kilmer to play Templar, but all notions of the *Son Of The Saint* plot were shelved and a new script portraying our hero as a high-tech thief and master of disguise was commissioned

**David Brown (producer), me with Lidia Lukes my Exec Assistant behind, Phillip Noyce, Phil Meheux (DoP) and Steve Harding (Production Manager)**

- it wasn't quite how Leslie Charteris had described him in the books! Nevertheless, writer Jonathan Hensleigh (who'd earlier penned *Die Hard with a Vengeance*), delivered a story about Templar being hired by a billionaire Russian oil and gas tycoon to steal the secret of cold fusion from an eccentric but beautiful American scientist. It was set to include London and Russian locations.

Paramount wanted to set the film up in the UK and invited me to join and oversee the production, but our first choice of studio - Pinewood - was very busy and MD Steve Jaggs said, "I just don't have any stages free."

So we went over to look at Leavesden Studios, which were then just a shell with converted hangars forming makeshift stages for the last Bond film *GoldenEye*, and it didn't impress us at all to be honest. As we were thinking about a Plan B, happily MD Steve Jaggs called me to say the Disney film that had been booked in to Pinewood was cancelled, so we slipped in quite happily.

**Val Kilmer and Elizabeth Shue on set in Moscow**

As I mentioned, the story was partly set in Russia and we were the first Hollywood movie to shoot in Red Square, Moscow. To say it was a tough movie, in all manner of ways from personalities to logistics, would be an understatement. When we first landed we were told that one of the Communist hotels was the only one available to us, and we'd all been booked in. There were gun carrying guards posted outside, supposedly for our protection from the Mafia the authorities assured us - that was all hogwash!

There was very nearly a riot amongst the crew, who declared the accommodation so bad that they would not stay there. I certainly wouldn't expect a crew to stay anywhere I wasn't prepared to myself - and this was certainly one of those occasions!

I made enquiries and there were indeed a number of Western hotel chains, such as the Hilton, available so I ordered we all move across to them the next morning after breakfast. Well, the meagre breakfast served was so awful that we all decided to leave without so much as a cup of insipid coffee.

**Phillip Noyce directing our stars on location in a pub**

Being an American production with lots of dollars to, shall we say, offer 'gratuities', opened an enormous amount of doors to us. If we wanted to close down streets, a few dollar bills to the right person ensured that they were cleared and cordoned off immediately.

In addition to Red Square we wanted to film in a hospital, a railway station and across rooftops of buildings. Again, a few dollars to the various authorities involved granted us immediate permission. Though we only had three weeks' shooting, the secret of pulling all this off was in having an especially long prep period in arranging all the 'permissions' and logistics well in advance of the main unit arriving. In fact Paramount queried why we'd scheduled so long, but soon appreciated how valuable the extra time and investment had been, and because of that, and the expertise of the production team, everything went swimmingly. Though there was one problem we encountered when shooting in Red Square; we had hundreds of extras for the big crowd scenes and our caterer, Robin Demetriou, reported all of his plates and cutlery hadn't been returned after lunch. They seemingly didn't have much at home in the way of crockery or cutlery, and for that reason we had to use paper plates and plastic knives and forks for the rest of the week!

One terrible sadness that befell the production was when our American casting director, Elisabeth Leustig, was killed in Moscow. She was knocked over by a car that didn't stop at traffic lights. The driver was never caught.

Our editor Terry Rawlings - who is one of the nicest and most competent men in the business - put together a rough cut a few days after we'd completed shooting, and I flew with him and director Philip Noyce to LA to meet with studio President Sherry Lansing.

Before landing in California, we sort of knew and acknowledged between ourselves it wasn't a very good film - it just didn't work in the way we'd hoped - but nevertheless we made our pilgrimage with high hopes and our heads held high. At 3pm the next day it was run in the theatre for Sherry, Philip, Terry and me. At the end, Sherry leapt up and said, "Philip darling, this is like a David Lean film!"

"Paul," she said to me, "you're a lucky producer. This is fantastic! We'll meet up later when we have the screening at 7pm for the invited audience."

Terry Rawlings looked at me perplexed. We suddenly felt incredibly excited and started saying, "Oh, maybe we were too close to it", then duly had a few drinks to celebrate.

Later that evening the film was screened, and when the score cards were handed in at the end we had the lowest score ever awarded to a Paramount film. The rug was royally pulled out from under us.

Paramount Chairman, Jonathan Dolgen, was in the theatre and once it emptied looked across and snapped at me, "I want you and Philip in my office at 11pm tonight. Make sure you're there I've got some things to say to you!"

"Yes," added Sherry, in a complete change of character, "we've got things to say."

We duly shuffled in to the executive offices at the designated hour and Dolgen said, "I've always thought the ending was wrong. Killing Elizabeth Shue's character was a mistake. We're going to re-shoot all that for her to live. How much will it cost?"

**Editor Terry Rawlings and me at the premiere**

I said a number, which off the top of my head seemed very realistic.

"It can't cost that much," he snapped.

I'd obviously failed to notice that he was a genius in budgeting. "Well you just asked me. We'd have to pay Kilmer for a start..."

"I'm not paying Kilmer for re-shoots," he interrupted.

"I know his contract. He won't re-shoot for free," I reasoned.

"I'm not paying Kilmer, do you understand?"

I said "Fine," and returned to the UK; and from there we re-wrote the ending, went out to Oxford and shot the extra material, cut it together and took it to LA to screen.

We were awarded exactly the same low score, proving once something is not right, it's very difficult to change it. And by the way, we did pay Kilmer to come back.

The score card thing has always puzzled me as a producer. When a studio pays millions to a writer, director, a big star to head the cast, and all the producers' fees... it's a huge investment and commitment. Then they're interested in the comments of someone who works for a fast food company on a weekend! If they don't believe in that talent why are they paying them all this money?

We could show (or sneak preview as they call it) a film tonight to an audience of fifty, and the next night to another fifty and you'll get completely different reactions and feedback, but on the back of it, a studio will order reshoots or a recut. That's always puzzled me. If you had a good script and team to start with, that's all you need to believe in. The Bond films never 'sneak' - they are released once the producers and directors deliver their cut to the studio.

The people who green light films are obviously to blame.

*The Saint* wasn't quite as bad as some suggested, and at an estimated cost of $68 million it just about recouped its costs, but with critical acclaim being mixed to bad I'm afraid all ideas of this being the first in a series of new film adventures for the character were well and truly scuppered.

A year or so later, Val Kilmer bumped into Roger Moore at the Cannes Film Festival and Kilmer told him that since making the film he'd started reading Leslie Charteris' *Saint* books. I think he must have finally grasped the essence of character because he said, "We really fucked that story up didn't we?"

LEONARDO DiCAPRIO
JEREMY IRONS
JOHN MALKOVICH
GERARD DEPARDIEU
GABRIEL BYRNE
For the honor of a king. And the destiny of a country.
The MAN in the IRON MASK
All for one.

# 1997-1998

## *The Man In The Iron Mask*

I was on holiday in Portugal when the phone rang. It was MGM's Production Chief, Bob Relyea, asking if I was free to do a film. I said yes, I was taking a break at the moment, but didn't have anything planned.

"I'll call you back tomorrow," he said, and hung up.

The phone rang late the following night, and it was Bob again:

"This is it Paul. We're delighted you're free. Can you be in Paris on Monday?"

It was then Wednesday. "Well, yes I suppose so. I'll get back to London first then fly over. What's the film?"

"It's *The Man In The Iron Mask*."

"Hang on," I said, "that's already shooting."

"Yes I know," Bob replied, "but we're firing the producer and we want you to take over."

I was a little hesitant, but then thought to myself that Paris is a very pleasant place to work so why not?

I arrived at the studios in Paris on the following Monday morning and realised they hadn't told the producer he'd been fired, as he was standing on the stage asking me what I was doing there. I told him I was taking over and suggested he call MGM and once word spread, the very next morning the French crew called a strike and said they didn't want the producer to leave.

**Leonardo DiCaprio, before.**

I realised going in heavy-handed and telling them that they were over schedule and budget in just two weeks wouldn't win me any friends and my position was made even more tricky when Jeremy Irons' make-up lady came wading in to the conversation saying, in front of everyone, "He was doing a fine job. He's a lovely man to work with and everything is going fine."

"I think it would be much better if you concentrated on Jeremy Irons' make-up, and let me decide just how fine and how on schedule and budget this picture is," I suggested. "I don't think you're in any position, sitting in the make-up trailer..."

With that, Leonardo DiCaprio came over, put his hand around my shoulder and said to everyone, "I think Paul is right. If MGM have made this decision, it's their money and their choice. Let's support him."

From then onwards it was a completely different atmosphere, and for this wonderful actor who must have only been in his very early twenties, to do that was something that I was not only grateful for, but it impressed me hugely; there aren't many Hollywood stars who would act with such maturity and foresight.

By the end of my first week on the picture, I'd brought over an American financial controller who'd been working at Pinewood on the latest Bond film for MGM, and together we reworked the budget and schedule to something more reasonable. The previous producer, no doubt under pressure from the studio, had fitted everything to a budget number, whereas in practice it is usually the other way around.

Having submitted everything to MGM I received a call from Frank Mancuso's office, the head of the studio, asking for all my credits and what qualified me to submit the revised (and increased) budget for his approval. Furthermore he was flying in to meet with me the following Monday with the express purpose of reducing the budget.

I remember we were filming on location in the grounds of a French chateau, Le Vicont, quite a way from the main house so you had to have a golf buggy to get around, and when I heard across the walkie-talkie that Mr. Mancuso had arrived I drove over to the house to greet him. He suggested we go to my office.

"I don't have one here," I told him, "but we can go to the catering tent."

Once there, he looked me square in the eye and demanded to know, "Who is responsible for this fiasco?"

"Your people, for hiring the wrong producer, and allowing an unrealistic budget to be signed off. But if you accept my budget we'll finish the film."

I also explained that the first-time director, Randall Wallace - who'd previously written the script for *Braveheart* - needed a little help and relied heavily on the 1st AD and his cameraman, so adding extra pressure on him to work quicker would, in my opinion, be disastrous.

"I'm going back to the hotel. I'll meet you tomorrow," he said.

At that next meeting, obviously having chewed it over, he asked: "Can you guarantee me if I give you the extra money you'll finish the film for not a dollar more?"

"I can't promise you that, as we might have the worst weather or someone might go sick, but I give you my word I will do my best to bring it in on time."

"Well you're not having a penny more!" he finished, and headed back to LA.

Unfortunately I spoke too soon about the weather, as for the first six weeks I was on the film temperatures hit a very humid 100 degrees Fahrenheit, making it very difficult, under the added heat from the large lamps, for everyone; but the following six weeks after the heatwave brought the worst period of torrential rain you can possibly imagine. So much that we had to lay down tracks and planks of wood over the sodden ground. It just goes to show that even with the best laid plans, you can't always count on the elements.

Waking up to hailstones the size of golf balls bouncing off the window sills didn't instil us with much confidence about the location filming ahead of us on those days, but ever hopeful that it would clear and we'd be able to turn the cameras, we left the unit base each morning and drove to the location... and waited, waited, waited. Occasionally there'd be a break in the clouds and we could start, but on other days we'd sit in tents and cars to no avail. DiCaprio became bored and frustrated - and who could blame him? - and I think everyone's patience and nerves were becoming very stretched.

**Leonardo, after. A very talented actor whom I very much enjoyed working with.**

Mercifully, we managed to complete the film and, dollar for dollar, it performed better than the latest Bond adventure, so we all felt quite satisfied, if exhausted, in the end.

Again those initial problems all stemmed from incompetent people trying to fit a film to a certain budget, just like with *Little Shop of Horrors.* Do the executives who green-light these things never learn? I know that's a rhetorical question!

TOM CRUISE
M:I-2
MAY 2000
www.missionimpossible.com

# 1998-2000

## *Mission: Impossible II*

After the success of *Mission: Impossible* I suppose it was inevitable that the studio would ask for a sequel.

When Tom Cruise was at Pinewood shooting *Eyes Wide Shut* for Stanley Kubrick, I literally bumped into him one day whilst walking through the covered way at the studio. He asked what I was doing next, said he was soon starting *Mission II* and asked if I might be interested in joining the production.

John Woo was attached to direct, and was another interesting choice on Tom's part as he was of course primarily known for directing martial arts films.

"The only problem is, John has his own producer, Terence Chang. Not that he's a hands-on type of producer, but out of courtesy I think you should meet them both."

A little while later I found myself on a plane to LA to meet John, Terence and Paula Wagner. John was a lovely guy but I really got the impression he wasn't interested in the business side of things, and didn't ask about any of my credits - he felt we were compatible and that was all that mattered... that and the film stock arriving on time.

We agreed a plan of prepping the film in LA and then we'd move to Australia, where the bulk of it was set, plus some extra location work in Spain to follow at the end; but, the one thing we didn't have was a script!

**Mision Impossible II - Recce in Spain with John Woo**

I was shown an outline story, which Tom wasn't very keen on, and was sworn to secrecy about the storyline. It gave me an idea of what we'd need to do, and whilst I was able to start hiring some key crew in Australia, I couldn't really progress things much further. Every day I went for lunch with John Woo - along with half the office who he invited and paid for - and every day that meant a full Chinese meal, but after seven months whilst we were waiting for a script to be delivered, I really felt I couldn't face another bowl of noodles and rice.

Paula Wagner told me Tom had decided he'd like a certain cameraman, Andrew Leslie, as our Director of Photography. Now, we'd already done some camera tests with Thandie Newton, to see if she'd be right for the film, and the cameraman on those tests had been given a six-week guarantee by the studio. However, having seen the tests Tom felt Thandie was perfect, but the cameraman was not and we'd have to fire him, to replace him with Andrew.

The cameraman was on a $25,000 a week, six-week contract, and I was therefore faced with paying him off with $150,000 for doing just one day's work.

Andrew flew to LA to meet with Tom, Paula, John and me. After a little while Tom excused himself and left the rest of us to sit in silence. Paula Wagner, although Tom's producing partner, never had any real knowledge about the technicalities of making a film, so when Andrew looked up at John and asked, "What sort of film stock will you be using on the movie?" John didn't quite understand the question, as he'd been used to his cameraman turning up and rolling cameras; the type of stock was never mentioned as long as it was high speed. Then Paula Wagner piped up, "Well, we want to make this film in colour."

Andrew looked at me, I looked at him... and just raised my eyebrows.

Next we headed off on a recce of the whole of Spain from Barcelona down to Malaga, looking for locations - for a film that we didn't really have a script for. But the idea was that it would be the place where the chemicals in the script were being developed, and I had the idea of the front being the vineyards with huge vats of wine, and behind being the factory. In the end,

**Tom Cruise and Thandie Newton, during an assesment of costumes**

John settled on some places we'd seen in Granada, so we appointed a local production manager and headed back to LA.

The next thing I knew, Sherry Lansing and Fred Gallo told me that they were not going to green-light the film unless we took $10 million off the budget. They wanted to try and bring the film in for under $100 million, but the point they didn't really appreciate - which I tried to make - was we didn't have a final budget, as we didn't have a script. It was 'best guess' time. But they were adamant.

So, I told Tom that we had a problem in that we needed to shave $10 million off, or the film wouldn't go ahead.

Nothing happened for a couple of days, and when I was driving back to my hotel one night I started thinking about the approximate daily running cost of a film like this being $400,000, so that would mean five weeks out of our schedule. To achieve that we'd need to rip out a quarter of the pages in the script! It just wasn't possible.

**Jeffrey Kimball, our DoP, and me in Utah.**

**Filming with Dougray Scott and Thandie Newton in Sydney Harbour**

However, I thought, "If we don't go to Spain, we could save a lot of time and a chunk of money."

The next day I broached the idea with our production accountant, and asked Tom Sanders (the designer) if he felt he could find the locations we'd earmarked in Granada somewhere in Australia. Tom was fairly confident he could, and we worked out it would save around $9 million.

Two days later, Tom Cruise called me from New York saying he wanted to have a video conference to discuss progress, and asked Lizzy Gardiner, our award-winning Australian Costume Designer, and Production Designer Tom Sanders to join us.

In the conference room, Lizzy immediately put her foot in it by asking Tom about how he saw the character of Ethan Hunt looking. He described a sort of smart casual look.

**Tom on the bike featured in the big climatic chase, filmed just outside Sydney**

"Tom, if you want to look like that you'll stand out like a pair of dog's bollocks in the desert."

Now, Tom had insisted that he wanted to see us but we shouldn't be able to see him on screen.

There was a deathly silence, and I thought, "That's the end of Lizzy".

It must have been about a minute before Tom asked, "So what do you think I should look like?"

"You should wear the sort of clothes Steve McQueen did - designer clothes that look lived in. Once you have a very good jacket, once you have a very good top... that gives a certain edge and style."

"I think that's a very good idea, but we'll have to get wardrobe to wear them down," meaning they'd have to be washed a few times, stretched a bit to look used. We must have spent a hundred thousand Australian dollars on clothes and of course Tom didn't want to try on any that weren't 'worn down' which meant that we couldn't then return any to the stores that he hadn't tried on or didn't like. The crew bought all the lovely cashmere sweaters and designer shirts for $5 at the end of production!

But the 'look' was at least solved.

Then Tom spoke to Tom Sanders about the sets, stage space etc. and finally he said to me, "I believe you have something you'd like to discuss?"

"Yes. As you know I've got to somehow save $10 million on the budget. I thought of us not going to Spain..."

"Are you crazy?" he interrupted, "Are you crazy? You know it's very important for the film, if we don't go to Spain then it won't work as a story."

He was royally pissed off with me.

"I've spoken to Tom, who feels he can replicate what we need in Australia."

"Well I'm not having it," Cruise ended.

A couple of days later I got a message from Paula that Tom was OK with us not going to Spain, and the next thing I knew Sherry Lansing was telling me how pleased she was.

The script was now supposedly 'just a couple of weeks away' from being completed, so the production manager, myself, Lidia and our accountant all shipped out to Sydney to set ourselves up. Weeks and weeks and weeks went by. We had three writers: one in LA and two others in separate locations in Sydney all working on it. We had stages pencilled in at the studio, actors were being contracted, but we were no nearer starting.

When the script finally arrived, we swung into action and started shooting. It was all going quite well until Tom Cruise told us he was unhappy with cameraman Andrew Leslie's work.

"I want to change him," he told me.

**My friend and editor extrodinaire Stuart Baird, just prior to him joining MI2**

"This ain't going to be easy Tom. He's an Australian cameraman, with an Australian crew, gaffer and electricians. They won't like it."

"Get me a list of people who are available," Tom said.

So, I produced some names of - American - directors of photography and Tom settled on Jeffrey L. Kimball, who was a very good old-time cameraman.

I went to see the union people who said, "No way."

Unfortunately for me, the Australian unions at that time were all-powerful, much like they had been in the UK a few decades earlier, and they were undoubtedly the biggest pain any film-maker had to contend with on the whole continent.

After much discussion, I persuaded them that it was the only way this movie was going to be completed as I'd otherwise be forced to close it down,

**Arthur Anderson, 1st AD, and me on the Bear Island location in Sydney, Australia**

**This is from the opening scene of the movie, with Tom Cruise literally hanging from a rock in Utah**

which would result in all the Australian crew losing their jobs, along with the many more millions we were anticipating spending in the local economy disappearing back to LA.

Jeffrey Kimball asked that he could bring along his own focus puller, who he was used to collaborating with, as he realised there would be so much high-speed action he'd need someone able to work quickly. I must admit some of Andrew's material which he'd shot was out of focus, as John Woo never worried about actors hitting their marks - he just kept the action moving.

Of course bringing in an American focus puller added a few extra headaches with the unions, but I took it on my shoulders as I did, telling Andrew that it was my decision to remove him from the picture. My shoulders are pretty broad. It was also my idea, so they told me, that the original Australian production designer they'd hired - before I joined the production - should leave in favour of Tom Sanders too. Firing people is not one of the aspects of my job which I like, nor did it make me very popular.

Incidentally, Andrew Leslie went on to win an Oscar for *Lord Of The Rings.*

With the start of filming fast approaching Paula Wagner asked me, "Is every job filled now Paul?" as she looked down the crew list.

"Yes I believe so," I replied.

"Hang on," she said, "who is this person here you've got down as Tom's stand-in?"

"He's a guy we looked at, he's Tom's height and that's what he does for a living."

"Well he won't be acceptable to Tom," she said, "as he definitely wants the same person that he had on *Eyes Wide Shut* because Tom said he was wonderful."

Now a stand-in essentially stands on set when the camera team are lighting a shot, to save the artist having to hang around unnecessarily. It's not a particularly demanding or difficult job. So I reasoned, "Flying someone in from London to stay here for the whole shoot will be very expensive."

"Well you'll have to make it work!"

"Who was he Paula? What was his name?"

"I've no idea... but he was very good."

As luck would have it, our production accountant had also been on *Eyes Wide Shut* so I popped across to see him, and asked, "Who was Tom's stand-in?"

"Oh, Tom never had a stand-in," he replied, "we just used the clapper loader."

Certainly Stanley Kubrick wouldn't have wanted to pay a stand-in so that made sense, but I often wonder why I don't look 102 on occasions like this - the best stand-in in the business indeed!

Two days before we were due to start shooting, the most terrible storm hit Sydney. In fact 30,000 homes lost their roofs that night, and along with them a great number of the cars we'd secured - via product placement - for later chase sequences were destroyed and had to be replaced rather hurriedly.

Once things got underway it ran relatively smoothly at the studio until, I think about 2 or 3 weeks in, when Tom Cruise asked me how long an actor had been shooting with us. He'd been on set for about twelve days at that point.

"How much would it cost to reshoot those twelve days?" Tom asked.

"Four to five million," I replied.

I could sense that Cruise wasn't happy about something with the actor though he never told me what. Next thing I knew, Tom took him to one side, read him the Riot Act and all seemed to be resolved.

Another problem arose much later when Dougray Scott suffered an accident on a motorbike and damaged his shoulder quite badly. The insurers asked us to come up with variances on what we could continue shooting with him.

Next on the schedule was a car chase sequence, and as it was apparent that we wouldn't be able to continue shooting the motorcycle scenes with Dougray being laid up, the only alternative was to bring the car sequence with leading lady Thandie Newton forward - in LA.

John Woo, meanwhile, was blissfully happy just shooting. He didn't really concern himself with any of the problems or issues we had, he wasn't particularly interested to be honest. But that was John. He loves creating action, and that's why people hire him.

Over in LA we also built a big descender rig in one of the hangars at the airport, as we needed that height to film Tom jumping out of a building. He never shied away from stunts like that, nor did he from the rock climbing scenes at the opening of the movie, which were filmed in Utah, hundreds and thousands of feet off the ground. John Woo loved that sense of danger.

Ten weeks after wrapping, John Woo brought the first cut of the film to run at Paramount. It ran just over three hours and was, quite honestly, the most boring movie you could try and sit through. The lights went up at the end, and nobody knew what to say.

We were called in to the executives' offices, and on the way over Paula said to me, "We are in a state of shock." I then bumped into John Goldwyn, who was Head of Production, in the men's room, and he said, "This is un-releasable."

"We've got a big problem," I said.

So, in the meeting I piped up:

"We have to plan what we're going to do as we have dubbing dates booked, music dates booked... It's not as though we just have to take ten minutes out, we have to cut 80 minutes of this movie and come up with a releasable film."

Paula Wagner looked at me and asked, "Have you got any ideas?"

"Let me think about it," I replied, and we all agreed to sleep on it.

The next morning I called Paula and, seemingly devoid of suggestions herself, she asked me if I'd had any thoughts overnight.

"I think we should bring Stuart Baird in," I replied. Stuart was not only an old mate of mine; he is one of the finest film editors in the business and has a first class reputation for being able to 'fix' a film.

"Really? I'll mention it to Tom."

Having heard nothing back from Paula the next day, I called her again.

"I touched upon it with Tom," she told me, "but he's worried about the effect it might have on John Woo's reputation."

"Paula, we have *got* to bring this to a head. I consider John a friend and my business partner, but we have a problem here."

Another forty-eight hours went by and no decisions had been made, but then the next morning - a Saturday - Paula phoned me at my hotel and asked if I thought Tom would be able to meet Stuart Baird.

"I don't even know if he is available," I told her, "I haven't asked because there is no point unless you all want me to!"

"I'll talk to you first thing tomorrow," she said.

In fairness, the very next morning Paula phoned me at the crack of dawn to say she wanted to bike a script to Stuart's house that day, and asked if he would then meet Tom Cruise in the editing room on Monday morning. John Woo meanwhile hadn't even been brought into the conversation and knew nothing about all this.

So I phoned Stuart, and asked what he was up to.

"Just taking it easy today," was his reply, "how about dinner tonight?"

"No, I need to have lunch with you."

"Paul, I can't today..."

"Stu, it will be very beneficial to you and if you are my pal, you'll meet me."

He told me the name of a restaurant where I could meet him, over in Malibu, and when I arrived I found him deep in conversation with Mel Gibson, who was there with his family.

"Why don't you both join us," Mel said.

"No! We can't!" I replied, much to Stu's surprise, "I need Stuart to myself."

"What's all this about Paul?"

I told him, and asked he accompany me to the studio first thing on Monday morning to run the film and then meet with Tom at 9am.

"Your agent will get you a good deal, as we're desperate people!" I added.

The following day we met up, and having seen the footage Stuart said, "This is a massive job, there is so much footage."

Tom Cruise walked into the room at 10am, and held his hand out to greet Stuart. Stuart looked at him and said, "I thought we were meeting at 9am?"

I thought this was going to be a disastrous meeting!

Tom started explaining to Stuart what he wanted, and all the sequences that had to stay.

"If you know what you want, you may as well just go and sit with Chris Wagner (the editor) and tell him. You don't need me."

"What do you mean?" Tom asked.

"I thought you wanted me to come up with a cut which, if any good, we could move on from?"

Tom leapt up out of his chair, stormed out of the office and slammed the door behind him.

It got to about 11.30am and Tom returned, "I've thought about what you said Stuart, and you're right. Come up with a cut and we'll take it from there."

Stuart did exactly that. Along the way he had a couple of fallings-out with Tom, as he is a very strong character who will not stand being told how to do his job.

Tom knew Stuart had done a brilliant job, and although they would never be best buddies they respected each other - from afar. More importantly though, Stuart made a lot of money for the producers and studio when the film was released and that, despite all the headaches and hiccups, is all that really matters.

JEREMY
IRONS
PATRICIA
KAAS
AND NOW...
LADIES & GENTLEMEN
DE CLAUDE LELOUCH
THIERRY LHERMITTE ALESSANDRA MARTINES JEAN-MARIE BIGARD TICKY HOLGADO
YVAN ATTAL AMIDOU SYLVIE LOEILLET PATRICK BRAOUDE ET CLAUDIA CARDINALE
www.andnowladiesandgentlemen.com
"Piano-bar by Patricia Kaas" chansons extraites et inspirées du film Sony Music

# 2001

## *And now... Ladies and Gentlemen*

This was an independent film, in so much as it was not studio financed. A rarity on my CV! It also meant we had to work with a completion bond insurer, who essentially stood to put their own money in should it have run over budget; again that was a rarity in my working life as studios such as Paramount and Warner Bros. never involved bonders - they underwrote all costs themselves.

Director Claude Lelouch had known my colleague, Warner Bros. Business Affairs Executive Rick Senat, for many years, and when Rick retired after twenty-seven years with the studio in 2000, he became a freelancer and, ultimately, co-producer of this film, which Claude asked I also join as Executive Producer.

Claude, a French director and writer, had won international fame for his film *A Man And A Woman* in 1966, which went on to win the Palme d'Or in Cannes and two Oscars. This was to be one of his only English language films. We were set to shoot in France, Morocco and London, with a cast headed by Jeremy Irons; although I believe both Dustin Hoffman and John Malkovich had earlier discussed the role.

Claude worked with a very small crew, and worked fairly quickly - which pleased the completion bonders! - and I should explain that Jeremy Irons played a character named Valentin who was an international jewel thief, and one of the early scenes was in London's Bond Street at a high-end jewellers.

My assistant Lidia had a very good contact at Bulgari, and so was able to get us to film at their flagship London store. Another reason for shooting in London was to access some of the 'soft money' available to film-makers.

Our hero then decides - hoping to discover some greater meaning to his

**Prepping in Bond Street, me with the late Ivan Sopher.**

**In Cannes, getting into the spirit of things for the premiere**

**In Cannes with Rick Senat**

life - to sail around the world, but we learn although money can buy many things it can't buy health, and after passing out, he finds himself in Morocco where he is diagnosed with a brain tumour. There he meets a burned out jazz singer - portrayed by French singer Patricia Kass - who also has a brain tumour! And so begins a new journey.

The title, by the way, was derived from the yacht Valentin sailed, which was called 'Ladies and Gentlemen'.

I have to say everything ran smoothly without any great concerns, and once the film had been completed we heard that the Cannes Film Festival, feeling it a bit of an event for Claude Lelouch to shoot an English movie, wanted to show it as their closing film of the 2002 festival.

In all my years in the business, I'd never attended the closing ceremony of the Cannes Film Festival before, despite having been to the festival itself many times. It was quite something with the long red carpet, hundreds of journalists and film crews and all with a panache only the French could add. It's almost like the Oscars, but with style!

Me, on location at Dobris Castle near Prague looking for locations for The Phantom Of The Opera, first time round.

# 2003

## *Phantom of the Opera*

Andrew Lloyd-Webber's film of the smash-hit musical first came to my attention in the late 1980s, whilst I was still working at Warner Bros., and was in fact a project the studio was backing.

Joel Schumacher was attached to direct, and Andrew cited his use of music in *The Lost Boys* as being one of the contributing factors in him suggesting Joel for the job. Andrew, meanwhile, was producing and had been guaranteed total control by the studio. I accompanied them both to Italy, to set things up, and we ended up at Dino DeLaurentiis' old studio where it seemed it could all work, but cost was an issue; so we then went to Prague and found it more advantageous. Designer Rolf Zehetbauer joined us and set construction was underway. It was quite an elaborate design as Joel had always wanted to be able to pan around all the backstage departments in the theatre - right the way around in one shot - which meant we needed to join two of the stages at Barrandov together. No sooner had we started than Andrew's divorce from Sarah Brightman was being finalised and he became, understandably, tied up in the negotiations. Meanwhile Joel was hot property and was wooed away to direct a series of Hollywood blockbusters, leaving everything in hiatus.

Warner's pulled the plug.

**Emmy Rossum played Christine**

I never heard any more about it, and even when I bumped into Joel in Hollywood on occasions he never mentioned the project, so I truly thought it would never be made.

One day, in early 2003, I received a call from Andrew Lloyd-Webber's office saying they had bought the rights back from Warner Bros., were making the film as an independent UK production, and as I was involved with it originally he asked if I'd be prepared to join them and set it all up.

Andrew appointed a guy called Austin Shaw (or Austin Seven as we called him) to oversee his interests in the film, which was rather ironic as Austin hadn't ever made a feature film before, but it was made quite clear that Austin and I would be partners in making all the day-to-day decisions.

We began preparing the film at Pinewood, and whilst I liked Austin I have to admit I found it difficult working with him because of his inexperience. That and the fact Andrew was personally cash-flowing the production at that point really made me feel as though I'd had a pair of handcuffs slapped on me; it was going to be an expensive film with lavish sets and wardrobe, and we were having to make all of our decisions and plans based on the cash-flow that was going to be made available rather than simply advancing as needed, as I would with a fully financed film.

Andrew's people were meanwhile pre-selling distribution rights to the film all around the world in order to patch the budget together; the problem being that sales estimates were (as they still are today) primarily driven by names in the cast. We had Emmy Rossum signed as Christine, and whilst she had some solid acting credits under her belt she wasn't, alas, a 'name' as such, but she was perfect casting with her combination of a vulnerable, fragile beauty along with her classically trained singing voice. In fact, in preparation for the role, she took ballet classes and started polishing her singing for two solid months.

The male, and titular, lead remained uncast and that was the question all the distributors and sales people kept asking; "Who will play the Phantom?" Early discussions revolved around Antonio Banderas, but somewhat surprisingly Gerard Butler was later announced as having landed the role.

The amazing chandelier

The detail and work involved was awe inspiring.

Our budget was set at £50 million ($80 million) which although generous by British independent standards, was extremely tight for this film - the sets alone were going to cost £13 million!

One of the pleasures of setting the film up was that although Joel was demanding creatively, he listened to my advice regarding the cameraman, production designer, line producer, costume designer and all the key creative personnel I felt he should meet and interview. I told him my mantra was always to surround myself with the best people, and he agreed. He hadn't made a film in the UK before, so fortunately didn't arrive with any crew in tow. One of the things I've discovered in my years making films is that so often a director will fall in love with a certain cameraman, or designer and wants to use them on every single film he makes - regardless of whether they are the right person for that film or not.

Joel was very demanding about how the sets and costumes looked, as his background was in costume design, so he wanted to ensure he had the very best people to do them full justice and I have to admit, in all the years I've been working on films, this one undoubtedly had the most perfect crew; everyone from hairdressers, prosthetists, carpenters, electricians, runners... you name it. You couldn't fault a single aspect. OK, you might say you're not a fan of musicals, or you don't like Andrew Lloyd-Webber's music, or the concept of the show but I challenge anyone to find fault with the film itself.

One of the sad aspects for me was that Tony Pratt, our brilliant production designer, didn't get the accolades he deserved for the simple reason everyone thought we'd actually filmed in the Paris Opera House and not recreated it on a stage in Pinewood! The sets were so fantastic that no one believed they weren't real.

E stage proved perfect for the main opera house set (with the chandelier falling) as it has the old projection tunnel attached, which was built in the 1940s for back projection purposes, so we could open up the doors and Joel could use the tunnels (or small stages as they are now) to get 'behind' the sets and add great depth.

Joel and Andrew had a very respectful working relationship and though

**Swarovski was heavily involved in the movie, and featured in a shop on set!**

both strong characters, they never argued. Andrew took over my office at Pinewood, as he wanted a room big enough to house an electric piano (and to be en-suite), and I moved downstairs into the main production office area; to be honest we rarely saw Andrew, he was always around but would stand quietly in the background and let everyone get on with their jobs. The only exception was one occasion when Joel wanted to do something that was going to cost a little more money, and as I used to travel back and forth quite a bit to Andrew's HQ in Covent Garden I'd be the messenger on such things as this.

"No, no," said Andrew, "we don't really want to spend the extra."

When I returned to Pinewood, I told Joel that Andrew didn't really want to spend the extra money and Joel smiled at me, "Oh, just tell him to sell another painting!"

I had a very good working relationship with Joel, but I did stand my ground when I needed to as with this being an independent movie we had a completion bond in place with Film Finances, and as such they were breathing down my neck on a regular basis ensuring everything was on budget and schedule. We didn't have the freedom of being backed by a major studio, so we had to be cautious and it was tough at times. I remember one day Joel and I had a bit of a falling out, as he thought I was being a little too inflexible, but later that evening he called me at home and said, "Paul, you know I always hurt the ones I love." Nothing more needed to be said.

I guess in my position I'm part psychiatrist at times as I know there's no point ever getting into a fight; that resolves nothing, so you have to try and manoeuvre the personalities and reach a compromise.

Aside from one single shot of horses racing up the road the whole film was shot at Pinewood, which was terrific as we didn't have to worry about locations, and all the hassles of transport and such like, and we had total control over every aspect of the film.

Of course, if you've seen the stage show, you'll know the most anticipated sequence is that of the chandelier falling.

My executive assistant Lidia had a relationship with Swarovski and she did a deal on all the jewellery, the costumes (which were encrusted with Swarovski crystals) and anything else required.

THE FILM.
The classic musical comes to the big screen for the first time.
A Joel Schumacher Film
Andrew Lloyd Webber's
The PHANTOM of the OPERA
Warner Bros. Pictures Presents
In Association With Odyssey Entertainment A Really Useful Films/Scion Films Production A Film By Joel Schumacher
"Andrew Lloyd Webber's The Phantom of the Opera" Starring Gerard Butler Emmy Rossum Patrick Wilson Miranda Richardson
And Minnie Driver Andrew Lloyd Webber Charles Hart Richard Stilgoe 'Le Fantôme De L'Opéra' by Gaston Leroux
Cameron Mackintosh & The Really Useful Group Harold Prince Nigel Wright Simon Lee Peter Darling
Nathan McGuinness Alexandra Byrne Terry Rawlings, A.C.E. Anthony Pratt John Mathieson Eli Richbourg
Austin Shaw Paul Hitchcock Louise Goodsill Ralph Kamp Jeff Abberley Julia Blackman Keith Cousins Andrew Lloyd Webber
Andrew Lloyd Webber & Joel Schumacher Joel Schumacher
WARNER BROS. PICTURES
DECEMBER

**One of the many Pinewood backlot exteriors we build for the film**

"What are you doing about the chandelier?" Lidia asked.

Tony Pratt and Joel both agreed it had to be a real crystal one. With all our incredible sets we couldn't cut corners with some plastic construction. Joel was also keen to see the myriad of colours reflecting in them too.

Lidia smiled and invited Nadja Swarovski, VP of International Communications, down and she agreed to finance and build the chandelier - at a cost of $800,000. It was going to be the heaviest ever made, was constructed in Paris and was shipped across in sections to be reassembled at the studio. There were three in total - a full sized, a 2/3 sized and a 1/3 size for achieving different shots, plus a mock-up for the actual crash - as we couldn't destroy the real crystal. Of course we had to strengthen the roof of E stage too.

It was the ultimate product placement as far as I was concerned and saved us a fortune.

It was so huge that Miss Swarovski hoped to later sell it to a grand hotel as a centrepiece in their building; it was certainly too big to attempt installing it in a more modest building.

All of the songs in the film were pre-recorded, which is normal practice

**Minnie Driver in full costume**

in musicals, but as we neared the end we realised there was no end music - as there was no song played at the end of the theatre show. Joel and I went to see Andrew on the Monday afternoon in Covent Garden and he said, "Well I'll have to write something."

On Friday of that week we visited his office and he played us what he'd composed, *Love Never Ends.* He was quite amazing coming up with something in such a short space of time.

The film had been greatly anticipated in many quarters, and certainly everyone who worked on it had huge expectations as it was so beautiful and we were riding on the back of the most financially successful theatre show in history. However, sadly, the film received a mixed critical and commercial reception.

Warner Bros. had stepped in to take domestic distribution and committed to $15 million for marketing, but other territories seemed underexploited and undersold to outside eyes, and I can't help but think the casting was partly to blame. Gerard Butler was not first choice; I don't think he lent the clout we needed for a film of this size and with Emmy being a relative unknown, despite being perfectly cast, it really fell to Gerard to carry the film - and that never happened.

Consequently most of the publicity fell on the shoulders of Andrew Lloyd-Webber, and as brilliant as Andrew is you really do need an A-list star to sell a film. During the rounds of TV shows Andrew mentioned he intended to follow with a film of *Sunset Boulevard* but alas, with a gross of $154 million worldwide *Phantom* only just about recouped its costs and would have given anyone cold feet about investing in a follow-up project.

It reminded me of *Greystoke* in a way. It was well made, everyone gave their best, it was an interesting story and was *nearly* a very good film - just not quite.

# 2005

## *Red Circle (Cancelled film)*

French production house StudioCanal announced they were going to remake Jean-Pierre Melville's classic 1970 film noir *Le Cercle Rouge* as an English language film, and its title translated to *The Red Circle.*

The original starred Alain Delon and centered on a thief who is released from prison the same day a murderer escapes police custody. The outlaws pair up and commit a heist as the cops close in.

John Woo was signed as director, and in all fairness I thought it was the sort of film John would do very well - lots of action, car chases, fighting etc. It was all going to film in the UK and I was invited to join the film and set it all up.

Unfortunately we didn't have a finished script, and so the nightmare began!

I flew to LA to meet John initially and he had some wonderful ideas. There was one sequence in the storyline where the two guys are being chased through a quaint old English village and John said, "It would be good if car go through pub, through conservatory like this..." and with model cars he showed us how he'd do it. Now I'd lived with John and his ideas through *Mission: Impossible 2* and that was all well and good because that was a big budget studio production with Tom Cruise; this on the other hand was a modest French production without Mr. Cruise!

However, when you sign John Woo you hire him for a reason and so I started looking at possible locations and costing up sequences.

StudioCanal immediately jumped on my back and started lecturing me about how Working Title (whom they co-produced some films with in the UK, such as *Notting Hill* and *Love Actually*) would "never spend this sort of money on this sort of film".

"Working Title wouldn't hire John Woo!" I replied. "He is going to make a very good commercial movie."

But they wouldn't have it, and beat me up over everything - we had to reduce the budget, cut scenes (despite still not having a full script) and in the end it seemed as though they just wanted to take all the action out of it. John Woo, by his own admission, is not a director best suited to dialogue-heavy dramas - he's an action director - so it seemed completely bizarre that they should want to turn their production into something John would be very unhappy directing.

I knew full well during *MI2* how bored John would get in scenes with Tom and Thandie Newton just talking; he wanted them to do it on motorbikes jumping over buildings.

StudioCanal fell out with John, then fell out with me and started questioning why we were spending so much money in preparation despite knowing we had a full art department, accounts department and production & locations managers hard at work; and we even shipped a huge model of the village we'd settled on to John in LA so he could play with his model bikes and cars and plot out the action... but the whole project was cancelled.

It's unfortunate that StudioCanal's aspirations exceeded their pockets and it was quite clear that they were not positioned to make big, international studio-style pictures. I felt so sorry for John Woo as the executives we were dealing with had no experience of being on a film set and consequentially no idea about what we were trying to do. Even when they ordered it all closed down, I explained that we had to put crew on notice (usually two weeks) but they argued that everyone should be fired there and then, and not be paid anything more.

I wasted the best part of six months of my life, and had a thoroughly unhappy, miserable time on the project, as I know John did. I've since read that John has mentioned resurrecting *Red Circle* in interviews he's given, but alas nothing has been confirmed at the time of writing.

Vince Vaughn as Fred and Paul Giamatti as Santa

Vince Vaughn with the Russian little people on one of the Pinewood sets

# 2006

## *Fred Claus*

The last major film I worked on was *Fred Claus,* which was a Warner Bros. picture based out of Pinewood. It was also one of the most unhappy experiences I had in the business, which no doubt contributed to my retiring soon afterwards.

When Warner's asked if I'd work on the film for them as Executive Producer, I unwittingly inherited a terrible mess, the first and major problem being nobody had come to terms with how to shoot it, after months of talking!

The story was about Santa's brother, Fred, who hadn't quite lived up to his brother's example but later was forced to move to the North Pole to help out with Christmas. So, consequently, there were a whole load of Santa's little helper Elves written about in the script. Most of them were going to have head replacements, meaning that well-known artists' heads would be superimposed, and it had been suggested that children be used for the bodies, which is absolutely ludicrous as they'd need hours in make-up, and with limits on working hours for under-sixteens it would mean we'd have them on set for about ten minutes.

I discovered pretty much immediately that the Line Producer had no experience of CGI (Computer Generated Imagery), the Production Manager had only ever previously been a Production Co-ordinator and this was her first film in this new capacity. It was not a good start.

I insisted the Line Producer - who is very much the nuts and bolts producer on the floor day to day - be replaced, which caused a lot of upset in the production office, and I was accused of being hard and horrible, but - and not wanting to say I was right in any conceited way - the lady went on to another film and was fired after just three weeks, then a third soon afterwards, making it a hat-trick of disasters.

I suggested if we could find little people, that would be the way forward but we'd need a lot. After scouring half the world, Lidia found a troupe of thirty such small people in Russia working in the circus. We flew them to London for the director to meet and screen test them, and returned them home. They seemed perfect for the job, so once production cranked up we arranged for them to come back, and billeted them all in a hotel in West Drayton, a short drive from Pinewood. The rooms had to be adapted with wash basins and wardrobe handles lowered etc., and we ferried them to and fro by mini-bus. On their days off they'd catch public transport and visit places like Windsor, Milton Keynes and Uxbridge but not once did any local press pick up on the unusual sight of thirty Russian small tourists getting off trains or buses. They really were terrific, and they never once complained about the long hours on set, but I have never seen anyone eat as much as they did. The notion of having an open buffet at lunchtimes was totally new to them, and they couldn't quite believe their eyes. They always tried to eat as much as they possibly could so they didn't need to spend their daily allowance on meals in the evenings; they all saved their *per diems* throughout and one of them, Victor, told me by the end of filming he had enough put by to buy a little car back home.

Although some of the small people spoke a little English, not all did so we felt it beneficial to bring in a translator in order they'd understand everything the director asked or suggested. It just so happened I was having lunch in the Pinewood restaurant that day, and when one of the regular waitresses served me, as I'd always been curious about her Eastern European accent I asked whereabouts she came from.

"Moscow," she replied.

"We're looking for a translator and need someone on the set," I told Lidia, "and I think we might have just found her."

She was a very bright girl and spoke perfect English. She agreed to move into the hotel with our small people and be on call throughout the shoot. From waitressing on tables, she suddenly found herself working on a huge Hollywood movie with hotel and a decent salary to boot.

Incidentally, six of the troupe - the ones that could speak the best English - later went on a PR tour of America and Canada ahead of the film being released. They had the most amazing time, and certainly helped generate lots of publicity.

Anyhow, back at Pinewood with filming underway I discovered the American producer, who'd also come up with the original story idea, had a ten-year-old daughter who sat on the stage every day with earphones on watching a monitor, and she'd chirp up with feedback to the director. I honestly couldn't believe it. There was a total lack of respect on the stage as a result, with no one person seemingly in charge - every decision was made after the trio of the producer, her daughter and the director watched the monitor and then asked star Vince Vaughn what he thought. Although director David Dobkin had worked with Vaughn on *Wedding Crashers* he seemed terrified of upsetting him, as did the producer. Whatever Vince Vaughn said they repeated as being exactly what they wanted.

My reputation as a straight talker obviously preceded me as I was told I was not allowed to speak to Vince Vaughn directly.

Complicating matters, the 007 stage at Pinewood where we'd scheduled to shoot a lot of the biggest sets burnt down, so we had to relocate to Cardington, a former airship factory which Christopher Nolan (a writer on this film) had used when directing *Batman Begins*. From there we moved to Chicago, and I'd earlier recce'd locations in the city with David Dobkin and for one particular scene I thought we'd found the perfect spot, only for David to say, "But there's a train going by behind us."

"There's very little dialogue David, so we could dub it [loop it] later."

"Vince doesn't do looping," he replied.

"He doesn't do looping? I've been in the business sixty years and have never come across an actor who doesn't loop dialogue where needed," I added.

"We'll just have to find somewhere that's quiet," he suggested, refusing to question his star's decision. I don't know if you've ever been to Chicago, but one thing it isn't is quiet. So we were faced with driving miles outside the city, and bang went an easily accessible location and lower cost.

Anyhow, the usual question came in from Warner's, "How can we reduce the budget?"

I'd already sent a few emails saying I felt we were shooting far too much material, and when Joel Silver joined the project as another producer (to help reduce costs) I suggested to him that as the script was quite episodic we could lose a few scenes very easily without impacting on the rest of the film.

"No, Vince Vaughn wants to shoot it," was the response we got back.

The director shot, and shot and shot. In fact there was so much material that ultimately there was more footage left out of the film than there was in it; but nobody would listen - except to the ten-year-old child who they constantly asked, "Is it funny, did you laugh?"

At one point, to hit our deadline of finishing in the UK before Christmas, seven units were shooting simultaneously. I've never in my life, not even on the biggest and most complicated action films, seen so many cameras and so much material coming into the editing rooms.

The director said it was imperative to do this as we were scheduled to fly across the Atlantic in order to "catch the snow in Chicago" immediately after the holidays; personally, as always, I felt had things been prepared differently and properly then this unnecessary expense would never have occurred as we'd have found a way of getting the essential footage in the can and moving on. But when you're dealing with a director who hasn't clearly formulated how they'll cut it together, and wants to cover every angle and eventuality as a result, then you're flirting with disaster.

It came together in the end, but what a headache it was getting it there - and it was a headache I decided I never wanted again. There comes a point when you know it's time to retire, and I felt I'd certainly reached it.

After spending six decades working in the film business and being very fortunate and pretty privileged to have known and worked with some terrific people, the idea of spending more time on the golf course and enjoying some winter sunshine with my (now) wife Lidia was made much more appealing by the end of *Fred Claus.* I have since been offered the odd film or two but have learned to first ask, "Who is directing, and who is starring?"

I'm in a position where, financially, I could afford to say "no thanks" - life is just too short!

# In Closing...

The film business is unlike any other: it's a hugely exciting and glamorous one involving very considerable amounts of money, but offers no actual guarantee of a return. What seems like a great script can, and does on occasion, turn into a disaster of a film in the wrong hands. And what seems like a bad script... well, you can never improve on it, but if the money is attached that seems irrelevant to most.

This is the only business that I'm aware of where the people in charge of making decisions have no actual experience of what they're doing - that is to say, making films. Whether they be agents, failed actors or just friends of friends, it seems to me that anyone can step forward nowadays to run a film company, and make multi-million dollar decisions. I suppose it's made easier when it's not their money?

One of my big bugbears is when a company heads to a studio like Pinewood, Elstree or Shepperton and happily block-books a whole raft of stages, thinking it's solid business sense, but as they draw nearer to production and the scripts have finally been written, they begin to release stages that they've now realised they don't need. Meanwhile, they've shut out other films that might have come in.

Does it matter? Surely a booking is a booking you ask? It does actually matter because when a film arrives in a studio it also brings with it a sizeable crew which set up in workshops, offices and construction units. They buy in materials from stores, engage on-site companies to become involved and inject a small fortune into the infrastructure and local area. When a big film block-books fifteen stages, yes it means they pay the facility, but it also means other films that might have shot there have been turned away - as has that knock-on revenue. Gone are the opportunities for employing two film crews, renting two sets of offices and workshops, buying in two sets of materials from local suppliers and so forth.

However, I realise that a new generation of people are now making films and indeed making decisions: and they work in the way they think is best. I'll just beg to differ!

I have greatly enjoyed the wonderful years I have spent in the film industry and, largely, look back with only fondness. I still love visiting Pinewood, and popping my head round a stage door when I walk past to smell that magical mixture of paint, timber and lights burning away filters. It really is quite magical and I'm so pleased to have been a part of it.

# Selected Filmography

Below is a list of major films which I either supervised or worked full-time on:

(Dates refer to year of release)

| Year | Director | Title | Lead Cast |
|---|---|---|---|
| 1964 | Lewis Gilbert | The 7Th Dawn | Bill Holden |
| 1965 | Clive Donner | Whats New Pussycat? | Woody Allen |
| 1965 | Ronnie Neame | Mr. Moses | Robert Mitchum |
| 1966 | Basil Dearden | Khartoum | Charlton Heston |
| 1967 | George Sidney | Half A Sixpenc | Tommy Steeele |
| 1968 | Lindsay Anderson | If | Malcolm Mcdowell |
| 1968 | Buzz Kulic | Villa Rides | Robert Mitchum |
| 1968 | Joe Mcgrath | The Bliss Of Mrs. Blossom | Shirley Maclaine |
| 1969 | Ken Annakin | Monte Carlo Or Bust | Tony Curtis |
| 1969 | Richard Attenborough | Oh! What A Lovely War | Colin Farrell |
| 1969 | Peter Collinson | The Italian Job | Michael Caine |
| 1969 | Michael Ritchie | Downhill Racer | Robert Redford |
| 1970 | Blake Edwards | Darling Lilli | Rock Hudson |
| 1970 | Lewis Gilbert | The Adventurers | Candice Bergen |
| 1970 | Vincente Minelli | On A Clear Day | Barbra Streisand |
| 1971 | Stanley Kubrick | A Clockwork Orange | Malcolm Mcdowell |
| 1971 | Ken Russell | The Devils | Oliver Reed |
| 1971 | Richard Sarafian | Man In The Wilderness | John Huston |
| 1973 | Herbert Ross | Last Of Sheila | Raquel Welch |
| 1973 | Lindsay Anderson | O Lucky Man | Malcolm Mcdowell |
| 1973 | Tony Harvey | The Glass Menagerie | Kathleen Hepburn |
| 1973 | John Houston | The Mackintosh Man | Paul Newman |

| | | | |
|---|---|---|---|
| 1974 | Tony Harvey | The Abdication | Peter Finch |
| 1975 | Lewis Gilbert | Operation Daybreak | Timothy Bottoms |
| 1975 | Stanley Kubrick | Barry Lyndon | Ryan O'neal |
| 1976 | Richard Lester | The Ritz | Jack Weston |
| 1977 | Michael Apted | The Squeeze | Stacey Keech |
| 1978 | Michael Apted | Agatha | Dustin Hoffman |
| 1978 | Richard Donner | Superman - The Movie | Christoper Reeve |
| 1979 | George Cukor | The Corn Is Green | Katharine Hepburn |
| 1980 | Richard Lester | Superman 2 | Christopher Reeve |
| 1980 | Howard Zieff | Private Benjamin | Goldie Hawn |
| 1980 | Stanley Kubrick | The Shining | Jack Nicholson |
| 1981 | Andrew Bergman | So Fine | Ryan O'Neal |
| 1981 | Peter Hyams | Outland | Sean Connery |
| 1982 | Fred Zinnemann | Five Days One Summer | Sean Connery |
| 1982 | Clint Eastwood | Firefox | Clint Eastwood |
| 1984 | Hugh Hudson | Greystoke: Legend Of Tarzan | Christopher Lambert |
| 1984 | George Roy-Hill | Little Drummer Girl | Diane Keaton |
| 1985 | Amy Heckerling | Nation Lampoon's European Vacation | Chevy Chase |
| 1985 | John Landis | Spies Like Us | Chevy Chase |
| 1985 | Richard Donner | Ladyhawk | Michelle Pfeiffer |
| 1986 | Harold Ramis | Club Paradise | Robin Williams |
| 1986 | Frank Oz | Little Shop Of Horrors | Rick Moranis |
| 1987 | Stanley Kubrick | Full Metal Jacket | Lee Ermey |
| 1987 | Steven Spielberg | Empire Of The Sun | Christian Bale |
| 1988 | Michael Apted | Gorillas In The Mist | Sigourney Weaver |
| 1988 | Roman Polanski | Frantic | Harrison Ford |
| 1989 | Tim Burton | Batman | Jack Nicholson |
| 1990 | Michael Caton-Jones | Memphis Belle | Matthew Modine |
| 1990 | Clint Eastwood | White Hunter Black Heart | Clint Eastwood |
| 1995 | Jerry Zucker | First Knight | Richard Gere |
| 1996 | Brian De Palma | Mission: Impossible | Tom Cruise |
| 1997 | Phillip Noyce | The Saint | Val Kilmer |
| 1997 | Randall Wallace | The Man In the Iron Mask | Leonardo Dicaprio |
| 2000 | John Woo | Mission: Impossible Ii | Tom Cruise |
| 2002 | Claude Le Louch | And Now Ladies & Gentlemen | Jeremy Irons |
| 2004 | Joel Schumacher | Phantom of The Opera | Gerard Butler |
| 2007 | David Dobkin | Fred Claus | Vince Vaughn |

23199201R00163

Printed in Great Britain
by Amazon